Especially for

_____

From

_____

Date

_____

A HELEN STEINER RICE ® Product

© 2011 Barbour Publishing, Inc.

All poems © Helen Steiner Rice Foundation Fund, LLC, a wholly owned subsidiary of Cincinnati Museum Center. All rights reserved.

Published under license from the Helen Steiner Rice Foundation Fund, LLC.

Text compiled from *Today* © 1991 and *This Is the Day* © 1993, both compiled by Virginia J. Ruehlmann. Used with permission.

ISBN 978-1-61626-485-7

Cover design: Kirk DouPonce, DogEared Design

Published by Barbour Publishing, Inc., P.O. Box 719, Uhrichsville, Ohio 44683, www.barbourbooks.com

Our mission is to publish and distribute inspirational products offering exceptional value and biblical encouragement to the masses.

Printed in India.

Daily Inspiration for Women

— THE BELOVED INSPIRATIONAL VERSE OF —

Helen Steiner Rice

BARBOUR
PUBLISHING

*H*elen Steiner Rice (1900–1981) has been called the "poet laureate of inspirational verse." The Ohio native worked as a greeting card editor before she began writing the countless inspirational poems that have been a favorite of readers for decades.

*A*s you start this year-long journey with the words of Helen Steiner Rice, you'll find that her beautiful verse will speak to your heart in a real and meaningful way. Read her words, meditate on scripture, and challenge yourself with devotional thoughts as you draw close to God and strengthen your relationship with Him.

A New Year

What will you do

With this year that's so new?

The choice is yours—

God leaves that to you!

Thou crownest the year with thy bounty.

PSALM 65:11

What would you like to see come to
fruition this year? What steps can you
take to achieve those goals?

DAY 2

Be a Light

You can't light a candle

To show others the way

Without feeling the warmth

Of that bright, little ray.

Light dawns for the righteous,
and joy for the upright in heart.

PSALM 97:11

How can you be a light of encouragement
to someone today? Who most needs
to see that light in you?

Say a Little Prayer

Games can't be won

Unless they are played,

And prayers can't be answered

Unless they are prayed.

The sacrifice of the wicked is an
abomination to the LORD, but the prayer
of the upright is his delight.

PROVERBS 15:8

What prayer is on your heart this week?
What is keeping you from
vocalizing it to God?

God's Treasures

All of God's treasures

are yours to share

If you love Him completely

and show Him you care.

We love, because he first loved us.

1 JOHN 4:19

How have you shown God to
your neighbors lately?

DAY 5

His Children

We are all God's children,

And He loves us—every one,

And completely forgives

All that we have done.

Train up a child in the way he should go,
and when he is old he will not depart from it.

PROVERBS 22:6

What guilt are you holding on
to concerning a sin that God
has already forgiven?

The Face of God

Accept what the new year brings,

Seeing the hand of God in all things,

And as you grow in strength and grace,

The clearer you can see God's face.

Both riches and honor come from thee,
and thou rulest over all. In thy hand are power
and might; and in thy hand it is to make
great and to give strength to all.
And now we thank thee, our God,
and praise thy glorious name.

1 Chronicles 29:12–13

How has God amazed you recently?

You Understand

You make me feel welcome,

You reach out Your hand,

I need never explain,

for You understand.

Welcome one another, therefore, as Christ
has welcomed you, for the glory of God.

ROMANS 15:7

How have you welcomed someone
during the past few weeks?

Only Love

Only love can make man kind,

And kindness of heart brings peace of mind,

And by giving love we can start this year

To lift the clouds of hate and fear.

Jesus answered him, "If a man loves me, he will keep
my word, and my Father will love him, and we will
come to him and make our home with him."

JOHN 14:23

Is your heart telling you to be kinder to
someone specific? If so, to whom?

Joy and Peace

Show us that in quietness

We can feel Your presence near,

Filling us with joy and peace

Throughout the coming year.

*"O my God," I say, "take me not hence in the
midst of my days, thou whose years endure
throughout all generations!"*

PSALM 102:24

How do you get focused for
a talk with Jesus?

The Great Story

Show me the way, not to fortune or fame,

Not to win laurels or praise for my name. . .

But show me the way to spread the great story

That Thine is the kingdom, the power

and the glory.

I have looked upon thee in the sanctuary,
beholding thy power and glory.

PSALM 63:2

How often do you look for opportunities
to communicate the gospel?

DAY 11

Cast Your Cares

No day is too dark

And no burden too great

That God in His love

Cannot penetrate.

Be not wise in your own eyes; fear the LORD,
and turn away from evil.

PROVERBS 3:7

How do you maintain your trust in
God when times are difficult?

His Presence

May He who hears our every prayer

Keep you in His loving care—

And may you feel His presence near

Each day throughout the coming year.

The LORD is near to the brokenhearted,
and saves the crushed in spirit.

PSALM 34:18

When or where do you feel
God's presence the most?

Surrender

Lord, I'm unworthy, I know,

but I do love You so—

I beg You to answer my plea. . .

I've not much to give, but as long as I live,

May I give it completely to Thee!

Give heed to me, O LORD,
and hearken to my plea.

JEREMIAH 18:19

When was the last time you specifically
dedicated your days to God for His use?

Morning Prayer

Start every day

With a "good morning" prayer

And God will bless each thing you do

And keep you in His care.

Every day I will bless thee, and praise thy name for
ever and ever. Great is the LORD, and greatly to be
praised, and his greatness is unsearchable.

PSALM 145:2–3

Do you take time daily to say
good morning to God?

DAY 15

I Am Willing

Hour by hour and day by day

I talk to God and say when I pray,

"God, show me the way so I know what to do,

I am willing and ready if I just knew."

And I heard the voice of the Lord saying,
"Whom shall I send, and who will go for us?"
Then I said, "Here am I! Send me."

ISAIAH 6:8

How do you best hear from God?

Unchanging Love

In this changing world,

May God's unchanging love

Surround and bless you daily

In abundance from above.

But as for me, my prayer is to thee, O LORD.
At an acceptable time, O God, in the abundance
of thy steadfast love answer me.

PSALM 69:13

In what ways do you feel God's
presence during adversity?

Morning Meeting

If you meet God in the morning

And ask for guidance when you pray,

You will never in your lifetime

Face another hopeless day.

Sing praises to the LORD, O you his saints,
and give thanks to his holy name. For his anger is
but for a moment, and his favor is for a lifetime.

PSALM 30:4–5

In what areas do you most
frequently ask for guidance?

The Gift of Time

How will you use the days of this year

And the time God has placed

in your hands—

Will you waste the minutes

and squander the hours,

Leaving no prints behind in time's sands?

Behold, now is the acceptable time;
behold, now is the day of salvation.

2 CORINTHIANS 6:2

How well do you manage your time?
Are there extra minutes or hours
in your schedule when you could
be working for God?

Heir to the Kingdom

Thank You again for Your mercy and love

And for making me heir to

Your kingdom above!

The LORD is my strength and my shield; in him my heart trusts; so I am helped, and my heart exults, and with my song I give thanks to him.

PSALM 28:7

How do you praise God?

God Is Everywhere

God's mighty hand

Can be felt every minute,

For there is nothing on earth

That God isn't in it.

O sing to the LORD a new song, for he has done
marvelous things! His right hand and his
holy arm have gotten him victory.

PSALM 98:1

How do you keep God in the forefront
when things are going well?

The Golden Chain of Friendship

Friendship is a golden chain,

The links are friends so dear,

And like a rare and precious jewel

It's treasured more each year.

A friend loves at all times.

PROVERBS 17:17

Is God part of your closest friendships?

Strong Faith

God, help me in my own small way

To somehow do something each day

To show You that I love You best

And that my faith will stand each test.

I kept my faith, even when I said,
"I am greatly afflicted."

PSALM 116:10

What one act of kindness has
meant the most to you?

Rest Safely

All who have God's blessing

Can rest safely in His care,

For He promises safe passage

On the wings of faith and prayer.

I long to dwell in your tent forever and take
refuge in the shelter of your wings.

PSALM 61:4 NIV

In what areas of your life do you
need to "rest safely in His care"?

Brighter Tomorrows

Whatever our problems,

our troubles and sorrows,

If we trust in the Lord,

there'll be brighter tomorrows.

I trust in the steadfast love
of God for ever and ever.

PSALM 52:8

How do you feel when you
place your trust in God?

Do to Others

Each day as it comes

brings a chance to each one

To live to the fullest,

leaving nothing undone

That would brighten the life

or lighten the load

Of some weary traveler

lost on life's road.

Blessed be the Lord, who daily bears us up;
God is our salvation.

PSALM 68:19

During stressful or troubling times,
how difficult is it for you to reflect
God's light to others?

Praying for Others

I said a little prayer for you,

and I asked the Lord above

To keep you safely in His care

and enfold you in His love.

"If you abide in me, and my words abide in you,
ask whatever you will, and it shall be done for you."

JOHN 15:7

How fervently do you
pray for others' cares?

DAY 27

Childlike Faith

Faith in things we cannot see

Requires a child's simplicity—

Oh, Father, grant once more

to women and men

A simple, childlike faith again.

For we walk by faith, not by sight.

2 CORINTHIANS 5:7

In what areas of your life are you
in need of a childlike faith?

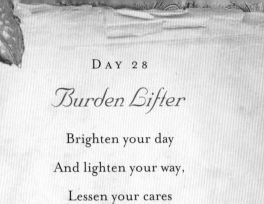

DAY 28

Burden Lifter

Brighten your day

And lighten your way,

Lessen your cares

With daily prayers.

O taste and see that the LORD is good!
Happy is the man who takes refuge in him!

PSALM 34:8

What cares are holding you
back from a bright day?

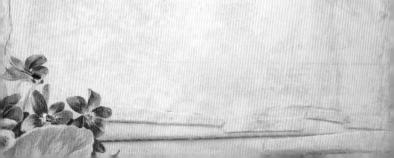

Invite God

Open up your hardened heart

and let God enter in—

He only wants to help you

a new life to begin.

Don't grumble against one another,
brothers and sisters, or you will be judged.
The Judge is standing at the door!

JAMES 5:9 NIV

Have you taken time to
talk with God today?

Teach Us

Give us, through the coming year,

Quietness of mind,

Teach us to be patient

And always to be kind.

I waited patiently for the LORD;
he inclined to me and heard my cry.

PSALM 40:1

What situations try your patience?
What can you learn from these?

DAY 31

Nearly and Dearly

When God forgives us,

we, too, must forgive

And resolve to do better

each day that we live

By constantly trying to be

like Him more nearly,

And trust in His wisdom and

love Him more dearly.

Bear with each other and forgive one another
if any of you has a grievance against someone.
Forgive as the Lord forgave you.

COLOSSIANS 3:13 NIV

Whom do you need to forgive?

Peace

After the night, the morning,

Bidding all darkness cease,

After life's cares and sorrows,

The comfort and sweetness of peace.

The LORD is your keeper; the LORD is your
shade on your right hand. The sun shall not
smite you by day, nor the moon by night.

PSALM 121:5–6

What sweet times of peace
have you experienced?

Hope's Rainbow

We know above the dark clouds

That fill a stormy sky

Hope's rainbow will come shining through

When the clouds have drifted by.

The light of the righteous rejoices.

PROVERBS 13:9

How often do you look for a silver
lining during times of frustration?

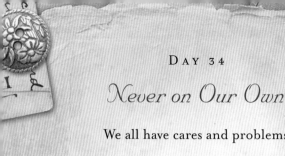

DAY 34

Never on Our Own

We all have cares and problems

We cannot solve alone,

But if we go to God in prayer,

We are never on our own.

A wise man listens to advice.

PROVERBS 12:15

When have you felt Jesus by your side?

Light vs. Darkness

God, in Thy great wisdom,

Lead us in the way that's right,

And may the darkness of this world

Be conquered by Thy light.

"I have come as light into the world, that whoever
believes in me may not remain in darkness."

JOHN 12:46

How is the darkness being
conquered by your light?

God Will Help

Let me stop complaining

About my load of care,

For God will always lighten it

When it gets too much to bear.

When the cares of my heart are many,
thy consolations cheer my soul.

PSALM 94:19

With what vices, such as complaining,
do you struggle?

DAY 37

Daily Miracles

Thank You, God, for the miracles

We are much too blind to see,

Give us new awareness

Of our many gifts from Thee.

One man pretends to be rich, yet has nothing;

another pretends to be poor, yet has great wealth.

PROVERBS 13:7

What blessings have you recognized lately?

Sympathy

God enters the heart that is broken with sorrow

As He opens the door to a brighter tomorrow,

For only through tears can we recognize

The suffering that lies in another's eyes.

*Why are you cast down, O my soul, and why are you
disquieted within me? Hope in God; for I shall again
praise him, my help and my God.*

PSALM 43:5

How did you encourage someone yesterday?

DAY 39

Small Deeds

Seldom do we realize

The importance of small deeds

Or to what degree of greatness

Unnoticed kindness leads.

He stores up sound wisdom for the upright;
he is a shield to those who walk in integrity,
guarding the paths of justice and preserving
the way of his saints.

PROVERBS 2:7–8

How have you definitely had an
impact on another by being kind?

DAY 40

Brand-New Start

It does not take a special time

to make a brand-new start,

It only takes the deep desire

to try with all our heart.

But he who looks into the perfect law,

the law of liberty, and perseveres,

being no hearer that forgets but a doer

that acts, he shall be blessed in his doing.

JAMES 1:25

What habits do you desire to change?

Daily Thanks

No day is unmeetable

If on rising, our first thought

Is to thank God for the blessings

That His loving care has brought.

Praise the LORD! O give thanks to the LORD,
for he is good; for his steadfast
love endures for ever!

PSALM 106:1

How has God been your
provider recently?

DAY 42

God Is There

There's no need at all

for impressive prayer,

For the minute we seek God,

He is already there!

"Pray to your Father who is in secret;
and your Father who sees in
secret will reward you."

MATTHEW 6:6

Do your prayers border on the
impressive or the personal?

DAY 43

Love Is...

Love makes us patient,

understanding, and kind,

And we judge with our hearts

and not with our minds,

For as soon as love enters

the heart's open door,

The faults we once saw are

not there anymore.

Love must be sincere.

ROMANS 12:9 NIV

Do you concentrate on others' faults?
How can you love instead?

The Mystery of Love

Love can't be bought;

It is priceless and free—

Love, like pure magic,

Is a sweet mystery.

Keep your heart with all vigilance;
for from it flow the springs of life.

PROVERBS 4:23

What is the best gift of love
you've ever received?

The Joy of Love

"Love one another as I have loved you,"

May seem impossible to do—

But if you will try to trust and believe,

Great are the joys that you will receive.

The wise of heart will heed commandments.

PROVERBS 10:8

How do you bring others joy by
showing love? Who in your life
is more difficult to love?

Tell Your Father

Remember, when you're troubled

With uncertainty and doubt,

It is best to tell your Father

What your fear is all about.

"For I know the plans I have for you,
says the LORD, plans for welfare and not
for evil, to give you a future and a hope."

JEREMIAH 29:11

What causes you to fear?
How does prayer help you
during those times?

Vision

Take me and break me and

make me, dear God,

Just what You want me to be—

Give me the strength to

accept what You send

And eyes with the vision to see.

But the Lord stood by me and gave me
strength to proclaim the message fully.

2 TIMOTHY 4:17

What dreams has God given you?
Where do you think He is leading you?

Everywhere Miracles

God's miracles

Are all around

Within our sight

And touch and sound.

Make a joyful noise to God, all the earth;
sing the glory of his name; give to
him glorious praise!

PSALM 66:1–2

How do you draw joy and strength
from seeing God's work?

Self-Awareness

Uncover before me my weakness and greed

And help me to search deep inside

So I may discover how easy it is

To be selfishly lost in my pride.

Pride goes before destruction,
and a haughty spirit before a fall.

PROVERBS 16:18

How can you be of service to a
neighbor or coworker today?

He Is Enough

My cross is not too heavy,

my road is not too rough,

Because God walks beside me,

and to know this is enough.

*"When you pass through the waters I will be with
you; and through the rivers, they shall not over-
whelm you; when you walk through fire you shall not
be burned, and the flame shall not consume you."*

ISAIAH 43:2

Are you walking with God as you should?
What in your life needs to change?

Kneel Down

God in His mercy looks down on us all,

And though what we've done

is so pitifully small,

He makes us feel welcome

to kneel down and pray

For the chance to do better

as we start a new day.

Answer me, O LORD, for thy steadfast love is good;
according to thy abundant mercy, turn to me.

PSALM 69:16

What events of yesterday would you
like to revise? With God's help,
how will you start afresh today?

Easter Miracle

Miracles are all around

Within our sight and touch and sound,

As true and wonderful today

As when the stone was rolled away.

*They were on their way to the tomb and they
asked each other, "Who will roll the stone away
from the entrance of the tomb?" But when they
looked up, they saw that the stone, which was
very large, had been rolled away.*

MARK 16:2–4 NIV

What can you do to consciously
remember the Resurrection in
times distant from Easter?

Keep on Smiling

Just keep on smiling

Whatever betide you,

Secure in the knowledge

God is always beside you.

The LORD is near to all who call upon him,
to all who call upon him in truth.

PSALM 145:18

Do you find it difficult to be cheerful?
How has the Lord brought joy to
your life this week?

Sow and Harvest

Seed must be sown to bring forth grain,

And nothing is born without

suffering and pain.

Now he who supplies seed to the sower and bread for
food will also supply and increase your store of seed
and will enlarge the harvest of your righteousness.

2 CORINTHIANS 9:10 NIV

What good has come out
of your past sufferings?

Love and Care

Be glad for the comfort

You've found in prayer,

Be glad for God's blessings. . .

His love and His care.

The blessing of the LORD makes rich,
and he adds no sorrow with it.

PROVERBS 10:22

For which of the Lord's blessings
in your life are you most thankful?

Faith to See

When our lives are overcast

with trouble and with care,

Give us faith to see beyond

the dark clouds of despair.

"Therefore I tell you, do not be
anxious about your life."

MATTHEW 6:25

When was the last time your
faith was stretched?

Reasons to Be Glad

Be glad that you've walked

with courage for each day,

Be glad you've had strength

for each step of the way,

Be glad for the comfort

you've found in prayer,

But be gladdest of all

for God's tender care.

Be glad in the LORD, and rejoice, O righteous,
and shout for joy, all you upright in heart!

PSALM 32:11

When—and why—did you first
desire to walk with Jesus?

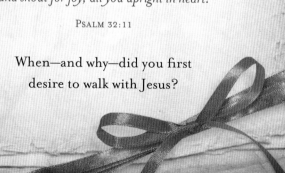

Serenity

May I stand undaunted come what may,

Secure in the knowledge I have only to pray

And ask my Creator and Father above

To keep me serene in His grace and His love!

"And whatever you ask in prayer,
you will receive, if you have faith."

MATTHEW 21:22

How much and how often do
you pray during adversity?

DAY 59

Wait

If when you ask for something

And God seems to hesitate,

Never be discouraged—

He is asking you to wait.

May integrity and uprightness preserve me,
for I wait for thee.

PSALM 25:21

Why might God be asking you to
wait for something you desire?

Better Tomorrow

God, be my resting place and my protection

In hours of trouble, defeat, and dejection,

May I never give way to self-pity and sorrow,

May I always be sure of a better tomorrow.

Every word of God proves true;
he is a shield to those who take refuge in him.

PROVERBS 30:5

When have you given in to self-pity—
and how did you defeat that
kind of thinking?

Spring Awakening

Flowers sleeping peacefully

beneath the winter's snow

Awaken from their icy grave when

spring winds start to blow.

So we do not lose heart. Though our outer
nature is wasting away, our inner nature
is being renewed every day.

2 CORINTHIANS 4:16

What untapped potential, forgotten
dreams, or unused talents are
lying dormant within you?

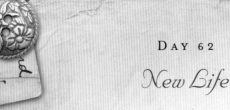

DAY 62

New Life

The bleakness of the winter
is melted by the sun,
The tree that looked so stark
and dead becomes a living one.

*Water will gush forth in the wilderness
and streams in the desert.*

ISAIAH 35:6 NIV

Has unforgiveness taken root in your
heart, preventing you from being
an example of Christ?

DAY 63

Unknown Friends

Widen the vision of my unseeing eyes,

So in passing faces I'll recognize

Not just a stranger, unloved and unknown,

But a friend with a heart that is

much like my own.

Then turning to the disciples he said privately,
"Blessed are the eyes which see what you see!
For I tell you that many prophets and kings desired
to see what you see, and did not see it."

LUKE 10:23–24

Are you quick to judge others?
How can you keep an open heart
and seek the truth instead?

Love One Another

Love works in ways that are

wondrous and strange,

And there is nothing in life

that love cannot change,

And all that God promised

will someday come true

When you love one another

the way He loved you.

"As the Father has loved me, so have I loved you.
Now remain in my love. If you keep my commands,
you will remain in my love, just as I have kept my
Father's commands and remain in his love."

JOHN 15:9–10 NIV

Which of God's promises are
you eagerly awaiting?

Meditate on Him

To understand God's greatness

And to use His gifts each day

The soul must learn to meet Him

In a meditative way.

To get wisdom is better than gold;
to get understanding is to be chosen
rather than silver.

PROVERBS 16:16

When do you like to spend time
with God and read His Word?

Faith and Love and Prayer

There can be no crown of stars

Without a cross to bear,

And there is no salvation

Without faith and love and prayer.

Blessings are on the head of the righteous.

PROVERBS 10:6

What is your "cross" to bear?
How can you reflect the grace and
glory of God through this time?

DAY 67

Trust and Follow

There are many things in life

That we cannot understand,

But we must trust God's judgment

And be guided by His hand.

*The LORD is a stronghold to
him whose way is upright.*

PROVERBS 10:29

Are you asking for God's guidance every
day, in every way? In which situations
are you trusting Him to lead you?

What Is Happiness?

Happiness is giving up wishing

for things we have not

And making the best of

whatever we've got—

It's knowing that life is determined for us

And pursuing our tasks without

fret, fume, or fuss.

There is great gain in godliness with contentment;
for we brought nothing into the world,
and we cannot take anything out of the world.

1 TIMOTHY 6:6–7

Are you living a contented life—
or a cantankerous one?

God's Mercy

Let us face the trouble that is

ours this present minute,

And count on God to help us

and to put His mercy in it.

The Lord disciplines the one he loves.

HEBREWS 12:6 NIV

Are you good at asking for help?
Are you better at giving help?

The Father's Creation

Our Father made the heavens,

The mountains and the hills,

The rivers and the oceans,

And the singing whippoorwills.

Let them praise the name of the LORD!
For he commanded and they were created.
And he established them for ever and ever;
he fixed their bounds which cannot be passed.

PSALM 148:5–6

What aspects of nature speak to you?
How do they affect you?

DAY 71

Life's Sojourn

Enjoy your sojourn on earth and be glad

That God gives you a choice

between good things and bad,

And only be sure that you heed God's voice

Whenever life asks you to make a choice.

"Today, if you hear his voice,
do not harden your hearts."

HEBREWS 3:7–8 NIV

How has God shown you the right path?

DAY 72

Your Name Is Included

God's love knows no exceptions,

So never feel excluded—

No matter who or what you are,

Your name has been included.

Let your face shine on your servant;
save me in your unfailing love.

PSALM 31:16 NIV

Can you brighten someone's
day by including him or her in
an upcoming activity?

Winning Life's Battles

Most of the battles

of life are won

By looking beyond the clouds

to the sun.

On the day I called, thou didst answer me,
my strength of soul thou didst increase.

PSALM 138:3

Are you in the practice of looking
to the Son for answers?

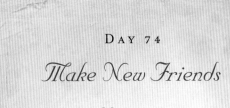

Make New Friends

May we try

In our small way

To make new friends

From day to day.

A faithful envoy brings healing.

PROVERBS 13:17

Are you holding on to some burdens
that you could give to God?

Live Today

Forget the past and future

And dwell wholly on today,

For God controls the future,

And He will direct our way.

A future awaits those who seek peace.

PSALM 37:37 NIV

What are you looking forward to today?
Tomorrow?

Count Your Blessings

Happiness is waking up

And beginning the day

By counting our blessings

And kneeling to pray.

Happy the people to whom such blessings fall!
Happy the people whose God is the LORD!

PSALM 144:15

How many ways have you
been blessed today?

The Risen Savior

In the resurrection

That takes place in nature's sod,

Let us understand more fully

The risen Savior, Son of God.

Rise up, come to our help!
Deliver us for the sake of thy steadfast love!

PSALM 44:26

What part of the Resurrection story
means the most to you and why?

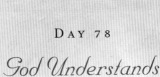

DAY 78

God Understands

No matter what your past has been,

Trust God to understand,

And no matter what your problem is,

Just place it in His hand.

"Forget the former things;
do not dwell on the past."

ISAIAH 43:18 NIV

In what ways do you want
to be more like Jesus?

A New Day

I see the dew glisten in crystal-like splendor

While God, with a touch
that is gentle and tender,

Wraps up the night and softly tucks it away

And hangs out the sun to herald a new day.

The sun shall not smite you by day,
nor the moon by night.

PSALM 121:6

When was the last time
you watched a sunrise?

Through God's Eyes

When we view our problems

through the eyes of God above,

Misfortunes turn to blessings,

and hatred turns to love.

"You will seek me and find me when
you seek me with all your heart."

JEREMIAH 29:13 NIV

What do you suppose God

thinks about your problems?

His Presence Is Near

God's presence is ever beside you,

As near as the reach of your hand,

You have but to tell Him your troubles,

There is nothing He won't understand.

Thou dost show me the path of life;
in thy presence there is fulness of joy,
in thy right hand are pleasures for evermore.

PSALM 16:11

Is God your first resource for help—
or your last?

Eternal Spring

Man, like flowers, too must sleep

Until he is called from the darkest deep

To live in that place where angels sing

And where there is eternal spring!

"For the hour is coming when all who are in the
tombs will hear his voice and come forth."

JOHN 5:28–29

What are you looking
forward to in heaven?

No Fear

Little brooks and singing streams,

icebound beneath the snow,

Begin to babble merrily beneath

the sun's warm glow,

And all around on every side

new life and joy appear

To tell us nothing ever dies

and we should have no fear.

For this slight momentary affliction
is preparing for us an eternal weight
of glory beyond all comparison.

2 CORINTHIANS 4:17

How has your attitude been lately?
Are you positively affecting others
or freezing friendships?

The Risen Savior

Shed Thy light upon us as
Easter dawns this year,
And may we feel the presence
of the risen Savior near.

"The Lord has risen indeed."

LUKE 24:34

When did Easter first hold
spiritual meaning for you?

Grant Us Grace

God, grant us grace to use

all the hours of our days

Not for our selfish interests

and our own willful ways.

And he came to the disciples and found
them sleeping; and he said to Peter,
"So, could you not watch with me one hour?"

MATTHEW 26:40

How often are you self-serving?

Life's Lovely Garden

Life's lovely garden would

be sweeter by far

If all who passed through it

were as nice as you are.

For lo, the winter is past, the rain is over
and gone. The flowers appear on the earth,
the time of singing has come, and the voice
of the turtledove is heard in our land.

SONG OF SOLOMON 2:11–12

Do you need to reconnect with a friend
or tell one how much she means to you?

We Live Again

Our Savior's resurrection was

God's way of telling men

That in Christ we are eternal

and in Him we live again.

"For this is the will of my Father, that every one
who sees the Son and believes in him should have
eternal life; and I will raise him up at the last day."

JOHN 6:40

Have you thanked God for His
eternal salvation and grace lately?

His Will

God only answers our pleadings

When He knows that our wants fill a need,

And whenever our will becomes His will,

There is no prayer that God does not heed!

"The LORD will guide you always;
he will satisfy your needs."

ISAIAH 58:11 NIV

Is your will in line with God's
about the things you desire?

Spring's Arrival

The sleeping earth awakens,

the robins start to sing,

The flowers open wide their eyes

to tell us it is spring.

*"Why is it thought incredible by any
of you that God raises the dead?"*

ACTS 26:8

What about spring makes you joyful?

A New Season

Flowers sleeping 'neath the snow,

Awakening when the spring winds blow,

Leafless trees so bare before

Are gowned in lacy green once more.

Like the crocus, it will burst into bloom;
it will rejoice greatly and shout for joy.

ISAIAH 35:1–2 NIV

What makes you "burst into bloom"?

DAY 91

Creation Speaks

Sometimes when faith is running low

And I cannot fathom why things are so,

I walk among the flowers I grow

And learn the answers to all I would know.

As you have heard from the beginning,
his command is that you walk in love.

2 JOHN 1:6 NIV

How do you relax and hear
God speaking to you?

Renew Me

You are ushering in another day,

Untouched and freshly new,

So here I come to ask You, God,

If You'll renew me, too.

Create in me a clean heart, O God,
and put a new and right spirit within me.

PSALM 51:10

When did you last feel fully refreshed
and renewed spiritually?

Goodnight

Who but God

Could make the day

And softly put

The night away?

Thine is the day, thine also the night;
thou hast established the luminaries and the sun.

PSALM 74:16

Are you a morning person or a night
owl? What positive things can
you find about the opposite time?

April

April comes with cheeks a-glowing,

Flowers bloom and streams are flowing,

And the earth in glad surprise

Opens wide its springtime eyes.

Be exalted, O God, above the heavens;
let your glory be over all the earth.

PSALM 108:5 NIV

When has someone brought joy
and happiness into your life?

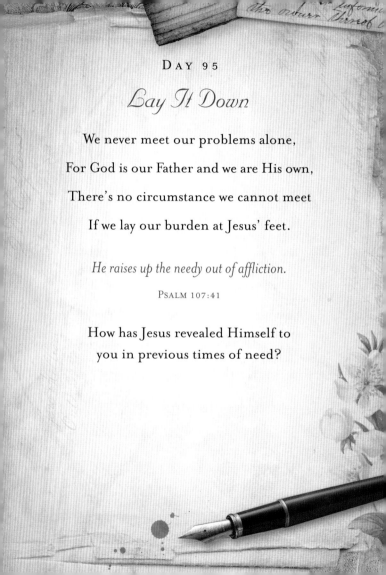

DAY 95

Lay It Down

We never meet our problems alone,

For God is our Father and we are His own,

There's no circumstance we cannot meet

If we lay our burden at Jesus' feet.

He raises up the needy out of affliction.

PSALM 107:41

How has Jesus revealed Himself to
you in previous times of need?

God Is Love

No one is a stranger in God's sight,

For God is love, and in His light

May we, too, try in our small way

To make new friends from day to day.

"Then the King will say to those at his right hand,
'Come, O blessed of my Father, inherit the
kingdom prepared for you from the foundation
of the world; for I was hungry and you gave me
food, I was thirsty and you gave me drink,
I was a stranger and you welcomed me.'"

MATTHEW 25:34–35

How can you reach out and
be a blessing this week?

God's Great Love

Keep us gently humble in

the greatness of Thy love,

So someday we are fit to dwell

with Thee in peace above.

And he said to the woman,
"Your faith has saved you; go in peace."

LUKE 7:50

Do you struggle with pride? How is the
Lord helping you with this weakness?

Rise Above

Like a soaring eagle

You, too, can rise above

The storms of life around you

On the wings of prayer and love.

"Therefore I tell you, whatever you ask in prayer,
believe that you have received it, and it will be yours."

MARK 11:24

When have you felt surrounded by prayer?
How has knowing that helped the situation?

DAY 99

Honor and Truth

Give us strength and courage

to be honorable and true,

Practicing Your precepts

in everything we do.

Finally, brethren, whatever is true, whatever is

honorable, whatever is just, whatever is pure,

whatever is lovely, whatever is gracious, if there

is any excellence, if there is anything worthy of

praise, think about these things. What you have

learned and received and heard and seen in me,

do; and the God of peace will be with you.

PHILIPPIANS 4:8–9

When do you find it difficult

to adhere to God's laws?

A Rich Harvest

Rejoice though your heart is broken in two,

God seeks to bring forth a rich harvest in you.

"While the earth remains, seedtime and harvest,
cold and heat, summer and winter,
day and night, shall not cease."

GENESIS 8:22

What areas of your life might
God be harvesting?

A Mother's Love

A mother's love is fashioned

After God's enduring love,

It is endless and unfailing

Like the love of Him above.

Serve one another humbly in love.

GALATIANS 5:13 NIV

How does your mother reflect
God's character of love?

Infinite Blessings

No matter how big man's dreams are,

God's blessings are infinitely more,

For always God's giving is greater

Than what man is asking for.

He will receive blessing from the LORD,
and vindication from the God of his salvation.

PSALM 24:5

Which of God's gifts to you were
greater than what you asked for?

Heart Gifts

It's not the things that can be bought

That are life's richest treasure,

It's just the little heart gifts

That money cannot measure.

"Give, and it will be given to you.
A good measure, pressed down, shaken together
and running over, will be poured into your lap.
For with the measure you use,
it will be measured to you."

LUKE 6:38 NIV

What "heart gifts" can you
give someone today?

Meet Each Day

Some work to do, a goal to win,

A hidden longing deep within

That spurs us on to bigger things

And helps us meet what each day brings.

*Let us run with perseverance
the race that is set before us.*

HEBREWS 12:1

Toward what goal are you persevering?

Blooms of Friendship

Friendship, like flowers,

blooms ever more fair

When carefully tended

by dear friends who care.

"Their life shall be like a watered garden,
and they shall languish no more."

JEREMIAH 31:12

What friendships do you
see blooming this year?

Divine Guidance

When we cut ourselves away

from guidance that's divine,

Our lives will be as fruitless

as the branch without the vine.

"I am the true vine, and my Father is the vine-
dresser. Every branch of mine that bears no fruit,
he takes away, and every branch that does bear
fruit he prunes, that it may bear more fruit."

JOHN 15:1–2

What fruit has come from
God's pruning of your life?

Many Blessings

The good, green earth beneath our feet,

The air we breathe, the food we eat—

All these things and many more

Are things we should be thankful for.

"As the heavens are higher than the earth,
so are my ways higher than your ways and
my thoughts than your thoughts. As the rain and
the snow come down from heaven, and do not
return to it without watering the earth and making
it bud and flourish, so that it yields seed for the
sower and bread for the eater, so is my word
that goes out from my mouth."

ISAIAH 55:9–11 NIV

How do you show your appreciation to
God for His blessings?

DAY 108

He Is Arisen

He was crucified and buried

but today the whole world knows

The Resurrection story

of how Jesus Christ arose.

They got up and returned at once to Jerusalem.
There they found the Eleven and those with them,
assembled together and saying, "It is true!
The Lord has risen and has appeared to Simon."

LUKE 24:33–34 NIV

How would you have felt as one of Jesus'
disciples after the Resurrection?

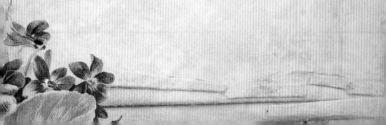

Changes

After the clouds, the sunshine,

After the winter, the spring,

After the shower, the rainbow—

For life is a changeable thing.

The LORD is my light and my salvation;
whom shall I fear?

PSALM 27:1

How is your life changing right now?
Are you accepting this change
or fighting it?

Divine Renewal

After the winter comes the spring

To show us again that in everything

There's always renewal, divinely planned,

Flawlessly perfect, the work of God's hand.

For the LORD is a great God. . . .
In his hand are the depths of the earth;
the heights of the mountains are his also.

PSALM 95:3–4

What might God be
renewing in you today?

Sun and Showers

God, give us wider vision to

see and understand

That both the sun and showers

are gifts from Thy great hand.

So if you faithfully obey the commands I am

giving you today—to love the LORD your God

and to serve him with all your heart and with all

your soul—then I will send rain on your land in its

season, both autumn and spring rains, so that you

may gather in your grain, new wine and olive oil.

DEUTERONOMY 11:13–14 NIV

How do you adjust to God's

unexpected or unwelcome gifts?

Forever Yours

Kings and kingdoms all pass away,

Nothing on earth endures,

But the love of God who sent His son

Is forever and ever yours.

But thou, O LORD, art enthroned for ever;
thy name endures to all generations.

PSALM 102:12

How has knowing God's unchanging
and constant love made a
difference in your life?

Our Father Knows Best

Our Father in heaven always

knows what is best,

And if you trust in His wisdom,

your life will be blessed.

And we know that in all things God
works for the good of those who love him,
who have been called according to his purpose.

ROMANS 8:28 NIV

How are you comforted by the knowledge
that God has things under control?

This Restless World

Everyone has problems in

this restless world of care,

Everyone grows weary with

the cross they have to bear.

And he said to all, "If any man would come

after me, let him deny himself and take up

his cross daily and follow me."

LUKE 9:23

What crosses do you see friends

and family bearing? How can

you help lighten the load?

Battles Won

Thank God for good things

He has already done,

And be grateful to Him

For the battles you've won.

"For the battle is not yours, but God's."

2 CHRONICLES 20:15 NIV

What might God be creating
in your life right now?

Relighted Faith

When you're disillusioned,

And every hope is blighted,

Recall the promises of God,

And your faith will be relighted.

Never be lacking in zeal, but keep your spiritual
fervor, serving the Lord. Be joyful in hope,
patient in affliction, faithful in prayer.

ROMANS 12:11–12 NIV

Which of God's promises can you turn
to when you need encouragement?

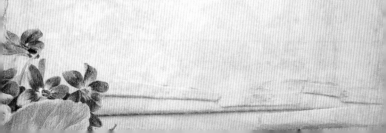

God's Purpose

God never plows in the soul of man

Without intention and purpose and plan.

*It is the hard-working farmer who ought
to have the first share of the crops.*

2 TIMOTHY 2:6

What good has come out of
God's plowing in your life?

The Anchor

God's love is like an anchor

When the angry billows roll—

A mooring in the storms of life,

A stronghold for the soul!

The LORD is my rock, and my fortress,
and my deliverer, my God, my rock,
in whom I take refuge, my shield,
and the horn of my salvation, my stronghold.

PSALM 18:2

How do you find God in
the storms of life?

Somebody Cares

God forgives you until the end,

He is your faithful, loyal friend.

Somebody cares and loves you still,

And God is the Someone who always will.

Bless the LORD, O my soul, and forget not all his
benefits, who forgives all your iniquity. . .
who crowns you with steadfast love and mercy,
who satisfies you with good as long as you live.

PSALM 103:2–5

What characteristics do you look for in a
friend? What kind of friend are you?

Blessings from Above

Each day there are showers of blessings

Sent from the Father above,

For God is a great, lavish giver

And there is no end to His love.

Thou art the God who workest wonders,
who hast manifested thy might among the peoples.

PSALM 77:14

How can you be God's eyes today?

Day 121

Disguised Blessings

God speaks to us in many ways,

Altering our lives, our plans and days,

And His blessings come in many guises

That He alone in love devises.

"The Lord bless you and keep you:
the Lord make his face to shine upon you,
and be gracious to you: the Lord lift up his
countenance upon you, and give you peace."

Numbers 6:24–26

How do you communicate to
your family that you cherish them?

Just Smile

You'll find when you smile,

Your day will be brighter

And all of your burdens

Will seem so much lighter.

I sought the L<small>ORD</small>, and he answered me,

and delivered me from all my fears.

Look to him, and be radiant.

P<small>SALM</small> 34:4–5

What makes you laugh?

Holy Plan

"Take up your cross and follow Me,"

The Savior said to man,

"Trust always in the greatness

Of My Father's holy plan."

God looks down from heaven upon the
sons of men to see if there are any that
are wise, that seek after God.

PSALM 53:2

Which aspect of God's character
means the most to you?

Why?

Why am I impatient

And continually vexed

And often bewildered,

Disturbed and perplexed?

Amazed and perplexed, they asked one another,
"What does this mean?"

ACTS 2:12 NIV

What frustrates you about yourself?

Strength for Today

God did not promise sun without rain,

Light without darkness

or joy without pain—

He only promised us strength for the day

When the darkness comes

and we lose our way.

You, LORD, keep my lamp burning;
my God turns my darkness into light.

PSALM 18:28 NIV

What positive things can come
from being in the dark?

In His Hands

God only asks us to do our best,

Then He will take over and finish the rest.

But be doers of the word, and not hearers only,
deceiving yourselves.

JAMES 1:22

What is your spouse's or
children's most charming quality?

God Hears

God hears every prayer

And He answers each one

When we pray in His name,

"Thy will be done."

"I desire to do your will, my God;
your law is within my heart."

PSALM 40:8 NIV

What service can you give
the church this week?

Holy Sunlight

Flowers sleep beneath the ground,

But when they hear spring's waking sound,

They push themselves through layers of clay

To reach the sunlight of God's day.

"Truly, truly, I say to you, the hour is coming,
and now is, when the dead will hear the voice of
the Son of God, and those who hear will live."

JOHN 5:25

What is making your heart
sing this morning?

Nature's Beauty

Thank You, God, for the beauty

Around me everywhere,

The gentle rain and glistening dew,

The sunshine and the air.

The eyes of the LORD are in every place,

keeping watch on the evil and the good.

PROVERBS 15:3

Where do you see beauty?

Infinite Blessings

God's grace is more than sufficient,

His mercy is boundless and deep,

And His infinite blessings are countless,

And all this we're given to keep.

"Ask and it will be given to you; seek and you will find; knock and the door will be opened to you."

MATTHEW 7:7 NIV

In what ways have you counted
your blessings lately?

DAY 131

Your Dearest Wish

Put your dearest wish in God's hands today

And discuss it with Him as you faithfully pray,

And you can be sure your wish will come true

If God feels that your wish will be good for you.

Thy hands have made and fashioned me;
give me understanding that I may learn
thy commandments.

PSALM 119:73

How do you help fulfill dreams
of your family and friends?

Help Me

Help me when I falter,

Hear me when I pray,

Receive me in Thy kingdom

To dwell with Thee someday.

One thing I have asked of the LORD, that will I seek after; that I may dwell in the house of the LORD all the days of my life, to behold the beauty of the LORD, and to inquire in his temple.

PSALM 27:4

How have you overcome past fears?

Forever Promises

Know that the promises of God

Will never fail or falter,

And you will inherit everlasting life

Which even death cannot alter.

Keep your life free from love of money,
and be content with what you have; for he has
said, "I will never fail you nor forsake you."

HEBREWS 13:5

When have you fallen short
on a promise you've made?

A Priceless Reward

Let me be great in the eyes of the Lord,

For that is the richest, most priceless reward.

The one who plants and the one who waters
have one purpose, and they will each be
rewarded according to their own labor.

1 CORINTHIANS 3:8 NIV

What are some acts for which
you'll be rewarded in heaven?

His Kind Benediction

When God sends sorrow

or some dread affliction,

Be assured that it comes

with His kind benediction.

"I will turn their mourning into joy, I will comfort
them, and give them gladness for sorrow."

JEREMIAH 31:13

Can you lend comfort to
a friend this week?

Be Still

Let us plan with prayerful

care to always allocate

A certain portion of each

day to be still and meditate.

"I will consider all your works and
meditate on all your mighty deeds."

PSALM 77:12 NIV

What do you love best about Jesus?

In a Flower

Little do we realize

That the glory and the power

Of He who made the universe

Lies hidden in a flower.

O LORD, our Lord, how majestic
is thy name in all the earth!

PSALM 8:1

What does creation tell you
about God's goodness?

DAY 138

Heart Vision

Love is unselfish, understanding, and kind,

For it sees with the heart and

not with the mind!

He who does not love does not
know God; for God is love.

1 JOHN 4:8

In what areas of your life do
you need to use your heart vision
instead of your head vision?

Brighten Your Corner

If everybody brightened up the

spot on which they're standing

By being more considerate

and a little less demanding,

This dark old world would very

soon eclipse the evening star—

If everybody brightened up

the corner where they are!

"You, LORD, are my lamp; the LORD
turns my darkness into light."

2 SAMUEL 22:29 NIV

What can be said about how you display the
fruit of the Spirit (Galatians 5:22–23)?

Silent Communion

Kneel in prayer in His presence,

And you'll find no need to speak,

For softly in silent communion,

God grants you the peace that you seek.

For God alone my soul waits in silence;
from him comes my salvation.

PSALM 62:1

Are you a peacemaker by nature?
How can you grow in this area?

Endless Love

To know life is unending and

God's love is endless, too

Makes our daily tasks and burdens

so much easier to do.

For the wages of sin is death, but the free gift of
God is eternal life in Christ Jesus our Lord.

ROMANS 6:23

How have you been given mercy?

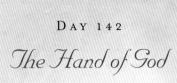

The Hand of God

In everything

Both great and small

We see the hand

Of God in all.

Arise, O LORD; O God,
lift up thy hand; forget not the afflicted.

PSALM 10:12

Where have you seen God this week?

Meditation Hour

Help us all to realize

There is untold strength and power

When we seek the Lord and find Him

In our meditation hour.

May all who seek thee rejoice and be glad in thee!

PSALM 70:4

How can you help a friend
strengthen her prayer life?

A Resting Place

The road will grow much smoother

And much easier to face,

So do not be disheartened—

This is just a resting place.

My people will live in peaceful dwelling places,
in secure homes, in undisturbed places of rest.

ISAIAH 32:18 NIV

How has your patience been tested lately?

Effective Service

Grant me faith and courage,

Put purpose in my days,

Show me how to serve Thee

In the most effective ways.

*Wait for the L*ORD*; be strong, and let your heart*

*take courage; yea, wait for the L*ORD*!*

PSALM 27:14

What ministry or service project
can you begin or renew?

Enduring Love

God's love endureth forever—
What a wonderful thing to know
When the tides of life run against you
And your spirit is downcast and low.

For great is his steadfast love toward us;
and the faithfulness of the LORD endures for ever.
Praise the LORD!

PSALM 117:2

How has the love of God or the
church surprised you in the past?

Happy Days

Spare me all trouble

And save me from sorrow—

May each happy day

Bring a brighter tomorrow.

"Look at the birds of the air: they neither sow nor reap
nor gather into barns, and yet your heavenly Father
feeds them. Are you not of more value than they?"

MATTHEW 6:26

How has God's love and care
brought you reassurance?

Higher Ground

In this world of trouble,

with darkness all around,

Take my hand and lead me until

I stand on higher ground.

When Jesus spoke again to the people, he said,
"I am the light of the world. Whoever follows me will
never walk in darkness, but will have the light of life."

JOHN 8:12 NIV

How do you feel when you help others?

Who needs your help today?

Opposites

Life is a mixture of sunshine and rain,

Laughter and teardrops, pleasure and pain,

Low tides and high tides, mountains and plains,

Triumphs, defeats and losses and gains.

For every matter has its time and way,
although man's trouble lies heavy upon him.

ECCLESIASTES 8:6

Reflect on your own life. In what areas
can you pinpoint the highs and lows?
What have you learned from them?

This Is Me

Each time you pick a daffodil

Or gather violets on some hill

Or touch a leaf or see a tree,

It's all God whispering, "This is Me."

Seek the LORD and his strength, seek his presence
continually! Remember the wonderful works that he
has done, his miracles, and the judgments he uttered.

PSALM 105:4–5

How can you use your
creativity for God's glory?

Forever True

When God makes a promise,

It remains forever true,

For everything God promises,

He unalterably will do.

And this is what he promised us—eternal life.

1 JOHN 2:25 NIV

What promises has God kept in your life?
What promises does He continue to keep?

Life's Ladder

As you climb life's ladder,

Take faith along with you,

And great will be your happiness

As your dearest dreams come true.

Love the LORD, all you his saints!
The LORD preserves the faithful,
but abundantly requites him
who acts haughtily.

PSALM 31:23

When in your life do you feel your
faith is the strongest? The weakest?
What have you learned from these times?

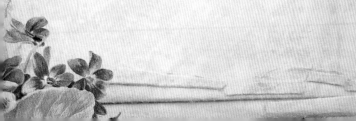

I Still Believe

Although I cannot find Your hand
To lead me on to the promised land,
I still believe with all my being
Your hand is there beyond my seeing!

*"I, the LORD, have called you in righteousness;
I will take hold of your hand."*

ISAIAH 42:6 NIV

How can you cultivate an atmosphere
of faith in your home?

He Never Changes

I am perplexed and often vexed,

And sometimes I cry and sadly sigh,

But do not think, dear Father above,

I question You or Your unchanging love.

Have mercy on me, O God, according to
your unfailing love; according to your great
compassion blot out my transgressions.

PSALM 51:1 NIV

How do you outwardly show
that you are devoted to God?

True Friends

When you ask God for a gift,

Be thankful if He sends

Not diamonds, pearls, or riches,

But the love of real, true friends.

A good name is to be chosen rather than great
riches, and favor is better than silver or gold.

PROVERBS 22:1

How can you show your friends your
thankfulness for their place in your life?

DAY 156

Let Him In

Open your heart's door

and let Christ come in,

And He will give you new life

and free you from sin,

And there is no joy that can ever compare

With the joy of knowing

you're in God's care.

"I am the door; if any one enters by me, he will be
saved, and will go in and out and find pasture."

JOHN 10:9

How can you spread the joy
of Christ to others this week?

No Night

I am faith and I am light,

And in Me there shall be no night.

God is light; in him there is no darkness at all.

1 JOHN 1:5 NIV

How can you make a difference
with a passionate heart for Christ?

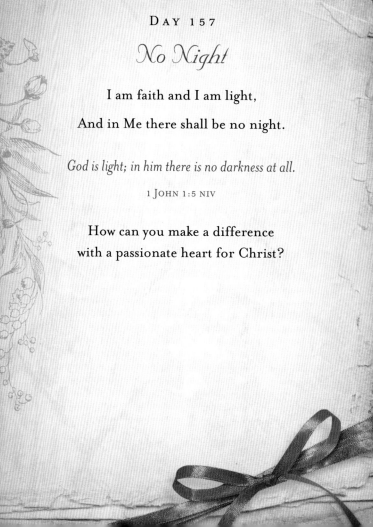

Add Sunshine

To live a little better,

Always be forgiving.

Add a little sunshine

To the world in which we're living.

If your enemy is hungry, give him bread to eat;
and if he is thirsty, give him water to drink.

PROVERBS 25:21

How can you shine a light outside
of your comfort zone today?

Grant Me...

God, grant me courage

and hope for every day,

Faith to guide me along my way,

Understanding and wisdom, too,

And grace to accept what life gives me to do.

Be strong, and let your heart take courage,
all you who wait for the LORD!

PSALM 31:24

When have you had to be courageous?

Near to Him

There is happiness in knowing

That my heart will always be

A place where I can hold You

And keep You near to me.

*Honor the L*ORD *with your substance and*
with the first fruits of all your produce.

PROVERBS 3:9

What is God saying to you today?

Wondrous Wisdom

God has many messengers

We fail to recognize,

But He sends them when we need them,

For His ways are wondrous wise!

Do not neglect to show hospitality to strangers,
for thereby some have entertained angels unawares.

HEBREWS 13:2

How have you shown someone a kindness
and become an unexpected blessing?

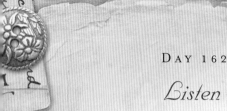

DAY 162

Listen

Teach me to let go, dear God,

And pray undisturbed until

My heart is filled with inner peace

And I learn to know Your will!

Every way of a man is right in his own eyes,
but the LORD weighs the heart.

PROVERBS 21:2

How have you previously known
you were in God's will?

Divine Assistance

Our future will seem brighter and

we'll meet with less resistance

If we call upon our Father and

seek divine assistance.

Surely there is a future,
and your hope will not be cut off.

PROVERBS 23:18

How can you provide hope to others?

It Takes a Mixture

With nothing but sameness

how dull life would be,

For only life's challenge

can set the soul free,

And it takes a mixture of

both bitter and sweet

To season our lives and

make them complete.

"Blessed be the name of God for ever and ever,
to whom belong wisdom and might.
He changes times and seasons."

DANIEL 2:20—21

How can you encourage someone today?

Unexpected Ways

God, make us conscious

That Your love comes in many ways,

And not always just as happiness

And bright and shining days.

I will come and proclaim your mighty acts,
Sovereign LORD; I will proclaim your
righteous deeds, yours alone.

PSALM 71:16 NIV

How did God's love on a really
tough day make a difference?

Treasured Friends

Often during a busy day,

Pause for a minute and silently pray,

Mention the names of those you love

And treasured friends you're fondest of.

The LORD has heard my supplication;
the LORD accepts my prayer.

PSALM 6:9

How does prayer abate your worries?

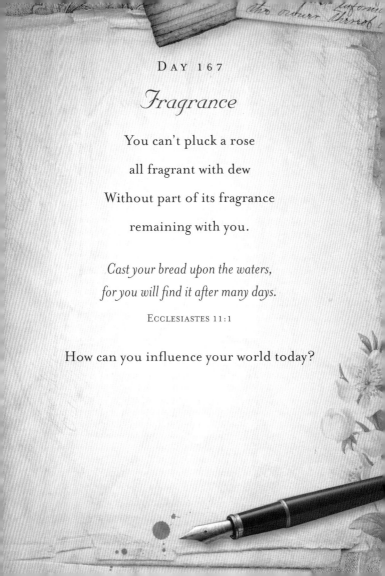

Fragrance

You can't pluck a rose

all fragrant with dew

Without part of its fragrance

remaining with you.

Cast your bread upon the waters,
for you will find it after many days.

ECCLESIASTES 11:1

How can you influence your world today?

He Holds It All

Somehow the good Lord gives

us the power to understand

That He who holds tomorrow

is the One who holds our hand.

If I take the wings of the morning and dwell in the

uttermost parts of the sea, even there thy hand

shall lead me, and thy right hand shall hold me.

PSALM 139:9–10

How well do you rely on God
and trust Him to guide your way?

Love Is a Journey

Love is a journey through the years,

With peaks of joy and vales of tears—

A journey two folks take together

Hand-in-hand through wind and weather.

"For this reason a man shall leave his father
and mother and be joined to his wife,
and the two shall become one."

EPHESIANS 5:31

How can you keep love alive with your
spouse through the ups and downs of life?

Kindness

Like roses in a garden,

Kindness fills the air

With a certain bit of sweetness

As it touches everywhere.

A gentle tongue is a tree of life,
but perverseness in it breaks the spirit.

PROVERBS 15:4

Do you struggle with taming your tongue?
Have you asked for help yet?

DAY 171

Timelessness

There is nothing that is new

beneath God's timeless sun,

And present, past, and future

are all molded into one.

What has been will be again, what has been done will
be done again; there is nothing new under the sun.

ECCLESIASTES 1:9 NIV

When have you felt God's
unconditional love?

When He Comes

The restless, unknown longing

of my searching soul won't cease

Until God comes in glory and

my soul at last finds peace.

"Peace I leave with you; my peace I give to you;
not as the world gives do I give to you. Let not your
hearts be troubled, neither let them be afraid."

JOHN 14:27

How do you get away to
relax and rejuvenate?

A Highway

Life is a highway on which the years go by—

Sometimes the road is level,

sometimes the hills are high.

I lift up my eyes to the mountains—where does my
help come from? My help comes from the LORD,
the Maker of heaven and earth.

PSALM 121:1–2 NIV

What have you learned from the choices
you've made this week—good or bad?

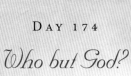

DAY 174

Who but God?

Who can see the dawn break through
Without a glimpse of heaven and You?
For who but God could make the day
And softly put the night away?

*For salvation is nearer to us now than
when we first believed; the night is
far gone, the day is at hand.*

ROMANS 13:11–12

What do you like about the dark?
Do you find it easier to be still and know
that He is God in the dark or in the light?

Angels All Around

Keep looking for an angel

And keep listening to hear,

For on life's busy, crowded streets

You will find God's presence near.

"Thou hast made known to me the ways of life;
thou wilt make me full of gladness with thy presence."

ACTS 2:28

What has been your
greatest blessing today?

Our Future

God, renew our spirits and

make us more aware

That our future is dependent

on sacrifice and prayer.

"And all these blessings shall come upon

you and overtake you, if you obey the

voice of the LORD your God."

DEUTERONOMY 28:2

What are some of your favorite hymns?
What effect do these songs have on you?

One Place to Go

There's but one place to go,

and that is to God,

And, dropping all pretense and pride,

We can pour out our problems

without restraint

And gain strength with

the Lord at our side.

For I, the LORD your God, hold your right hand;
it is I who say to you, "Fear not, I will help you."

ISAIAH 41:13

Where is your best "prayer closet"
to get one-on-one with God?

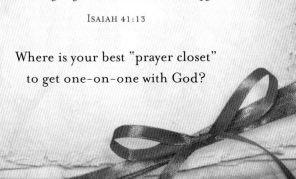

DAY 178

Take My Hand

Father, I am well aware

I can't make it on my own,

So take my hand and hold it tight,

For I cannot walk alone.

Though I walk in the midst of trouble,
thou dost preserve my life; thou dost stretch
out thy hand against the wrath of my enemies,
and thy right hand delivers me.

PSALM 138:7

Do you know someone who needs a
shoulder to lean on right now?

God's Whispers

Each time you look up in the sky

Or watch the fluffy clouds drift by

Or touch a leaf or see a tree,

It's all God whispering, "This is Me."

The heavens are telling the glory of God;
and the firmament proclaims his handiwork.

PSALM 19:1

How is gentleness exemplified
in the women around you?
How do you show gentleness?

Peace, Be Still

I know He stilled the tempest

and calmed the angry sea,

And I humbly ask if in His love

He'll do the same for me.

And he awoke and rebuked the wind, and said to

the sea, "Peace! Be Still!" And the wind ceased,

and there was a great calm.

MARK 4:39

Do you desire more peace in your life?

How can you better manage your schedule

to provide some downtime?

Let Go and Let God

Rest and relax and grow stronger,

Let go and let God share your load,

Your work is not finished or ended,

You've just come to a bend in the road.

Trust in the LORD with all your heart,
and do not rely on your own insight.
In all your ways acknowledge him,
and he will make straight your paths.

PROVERBS 3:5–6

What is causing stress in your life?
How often do you feel overloaded
and overwhelmed?

A Quiet Peace

Where there is love there is a smile
To make all things seem more worthwhile,
Where there is love there's a quiet peace,
A tranquil place where turmoils cease.

So faith, hope, love abide, these three;
but the greatest of these is love.

1 CORINTHIANS 13:13

What activity (in which you're normally
not interested) can you share with your
family that will show them your love?

Unexpected Miracles

The unexpected kindness

from an unexpected place,

A hand outstretched in friendship

a smile on someone's face,

A word of understanding

spoken in a time of trial

Are unexpected miracles that

make life more worthwhile.

Share with the Lord's people who are in need.

ROMANS 12:13 NIV

What is something unexpected
you could do today?

God's Open Hands

When trouble surrounds you

And no one understands,

Try placing your cares

In God's open hands.

Thou hatest those who pay regard to vain idols;
but I trust in the LORD.

PSALM 31:6

Do you struggle with pessimism? What are
five things you can look forward to today?

His Love Is Near

The earth is where we live today,

And we must serve God here,

For He watches us from way up there,

And His love is always near.

"But whoever would be great among you must be your servant, and whoever would be first among you must be your slave; even as the Son of man came not to be served but to serve, and to give his life as a ransom for many."

MATTHEW 20:26—28

As you admire the night sky, what do the heavens, with its stars, galaxies, and planets, tell you about God?

Endless Hope

I come to meet You, God, and as I linger here,

I seem to feel You very near—

A rustling leaf, a rolling slope

Speak to my heart of endless hope.

"From the fig tree learn its lesson: as soon as its branch
becomes tender and puts forth its leaves, you know that
summer is near. So also, when you see these things taking
place, you know that he is near, at the very gates."

MARK 13:28–29

Are you awaiting Christ's ever-near return
with hope? What will it be like to speak
with Him face-to-face?

Growth in Troubles

There's a lot of comfort in the thought

That sorrow, grief, and woe

Are sent into our lives sometimes

To help our souls to grow.

In the fear of the LORD one has strong confidence,
and his children will have a refuge.

PROVERBS 14:26

Where is your place of refuge?
How have you seen growth in
your life during times of trial?

A Reason to Rejoice

In trouble and in gladness

We can always hear Your voice

If we listen in the silence

And find a reason to rejoice.

"Then you shall call, and the LORD will answer;
you shall cry, and he will say, Here I am."

ISAIAH 58:9

How can you praise God
for what you see today?

Daily Blessings

We rob our own lives much more than we know

When we fail to respond or in any way show

Our thanks for the blessings that are daily ours—

The warmth of the sun, the fragrance of flowers.

All thy works shall give thanks to thee, O LORD,
and all thy saints shall bless thee! They shall speak
of the glory of thy kingdom, and tell of thy power,
to make known to the sons of men thy mighty deeds,
and the glorious splendor of thy kingdom.

PSALM 145:10–12

How can you recognize today
what you usually take for granted?

Teach Me

Lord, show me the way

I can somehow repay

The blessings You've given to me. . .

Lord, teach me to do what

You most want me to

And to be what You want me to be.

What shall I return to the LORD for all his goodness
to me? . . . I will fulfill my vows to the LORD.

PSALM 116:12, 14 NIV

How do you feel about your role
as wife, mother, daughter, caregiver,
and so on? What do you struggle with?
What do you enjoy?

He Is Aware

Our Father up in heaven

Is very much aware

Of our failures and shortcomings

And the burdens that we bear.

My flesh and my heart may fail, but God is the
strength of my heart and my portion for ever.

PSALM 73:26

How aware of God are you in your
day-to-day duties? How can you
become more aware of Him?

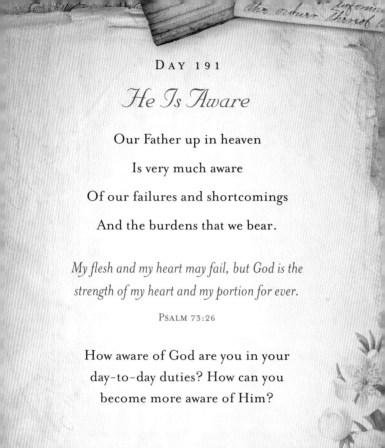

True Perfection

Wonder of wonders,

beyond man's conception,

For only in God can love

find true perfection.

The LORD is gracious and compassionate,

slow to anger and rich in love.

PSALM 145:8 NIV

Do you have a temper?

How does anger affect those around you?

He Gives Me Strength

If God does not ease my load,

He will give me strength to bear it,

For God in love and mercy

is always near to share it.

When you are in distress and all these things
have happened to you, then in later days you
will return to the LORD your God and obey him.
For the LORD your God is a merciful God;
he will not abandon or destroy you.

DEUTERONOMY 4:30–31 NIV

Are you a leader or a follower?
How are you at teamwork?

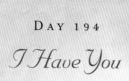

I Have You

My blessings are so many,

my troubles are so few,

How can I feel discouraged

when I know that I have You?

*"Be strong and courageous. Do not be afraid;
do not be discouraged, for the LORD your
God will be with you wherever you go."*

JOSHUA 1:9 NIV

How can you be God's voice today?
Who do you know that needs to
be encouraged by His truth?

Here Comes the Sun

Have patience to wait for the day

When the sun comes out

and the clouds float away!

The Mighty One, God the LORD,
speaks and summons the earth from
the rising of the sun to its setting.

PSALM 50:1

How can you make the world
around you a better place today?

Rich Blessings

May He who sends the raindrops

And makes the sunshine, too,

Look down and bless you richly

And be very near to you!

Thou hast fixed all the bounds of the earth;
thou hast made summer and winter.

PSALM 74:17

How can you cultivate an atmosphere
of thankfulness in your home?

Sweet Surprise

Make us more aware, dear God,

Of little daily graces

That come to us with sweet surprise

From never-dreamed-of places.

O my God, in thee I trust.

PSALM 25:2

What one word best describes
God to you today? Why?

Little Things

Little prayers for little things

Fly heavenward on little wings,

And no prayer is too great or small

To ask of God who hears them all.

Keep me as the apple of the eye;
hide me in the shadow of thy wings.

PSALM 17:8

What "little things" do you typically
not take to God in prayer?

The Peaceful Harbor

God's love is like a harbor

Where our souls can find sweet rest

From the struggle and the tension

Of life's fast and futile quest.

They were glad when it grew calm,
and he guided them to their desired haven.

PSALM 107:30 NIV

What Bible verse helps you to imagine
God being your harbor of rest?

There Must Be Rain

Our Father knows what's best for us,

So why should we complain?

We always want the sunshine,

But He knows there must be rain.

Do everything without grumbling or arguing.

PHILIPPIANS 2:14 NIV

What seemingly insurmountable task
can you ask God to help you with?

He's the Tree

We, too, must be dependent

on our Father up above,

For we are but the branches,

and He's the tree of love.

"Blessed are those who wash their robes,
that they may have the right to the tree of life
and may go through the gates into the city."

REVELATION 22:14 NIV

Imagine yourself in a peaceful,
quiet place. What is God whispering
to you in the wind?

Morning Meeting

The sun just rising in the sky,

The waking birdlings as they fly,

The grass all wet with morning dew

Are telling me I've just met You!

From the rising of the sun to its setting
the name of the LORD is to be praised!

PSALM 113:3

How often do you get to spend time
enjoying the outdoors or taking a walk?
Let your stress fly away and be
thankful for the exercise.

Reaching Out

Today my soul is reaching out

for something that's unknown,

I cannot grasp or fathom it,

for it's known to God alone.

Is there a thing of which it is said,
"See, this is new"? It has been already,
in the ages before us.

ECCLESIASTES 1:10

What would you like God to
make known to you?

It's Only a Bend

We stand at life's crossroads

And view what we think is the end,

But God has a much bigger vision,

And He tells us it's only a bend.

Show me the way I should go,
for to you I entrust my life.

PSALM 143:8 NIV

To whom can you show
the love of God today?

A Cheerful Attitude

If you'll only try to be cheerful,

You will find, without a doubt,

A cheerful attitude is something

No one should be without.

A cheerful heart is a good medicine.

PROVERBS 17:22

What brings you cheer in the summer-
time? What do you find to be cheerful
about in the other seasons of the year?

Wrapped in Kindness

If you practice kindness

In all you say and do,

The Lord will wrap His kindness

Around your heart and you.

He who pursues righteousness and
kindness will find life and honor.

PROVERBS 21:21

How can you encourage your
husband or children this week?

A Prayer for You

Here is a prayer for you

That you'll walk with God every day,

Remembering always in whatever you do,

There is only one true, righteous way.

"And I will walk among you, and will be your
God, and you shall be my people."

LEVITICUS 26:12

Do you know of someone who needs
a closer relationship with the Lord?
Pray for that person today.

My Cathedral

My garden beautifies my yard

and adds fragrance to the air,

But it is also my cathedral

and my quiet place of prayer.

And they heard the sound of the LORD God
walking in the garden in the cool of the day.

GENESIS 3:8

Where in God's creation do you
find inspiration? Why?

Walk in Love

Love changes darkness into light

And makes the heart take wingless flight—

Oh, blessed are they who walk in love,

They also walk with God above.

Love bears all things, believes all things,
hopes all things, endures all things.

1 CORINTHIANS 13:7

Whom can you touch with
God's comfort today?

A Heaven–Sent Gift

Happiness is giving up thoughts

That breed discontent

And accepting what comes

As a gift heaven sent.

He who gives heed to the word will prosper,
and happy is he who trusts in the LORD.

PROVERBS 16:20

What thoughts of discontent
do you need to give up today?

Trust Him

Deal only with the present

Never step into tomorrow,

For God asks us just to trust in Him

And to never borrow sorrow.

Yea, our heart is glad in him,
because we trust in his holy name.

PSALM 33:21

Do you worry about pleasing others?
How can you remind yourself to look
to God for acceptance instead?

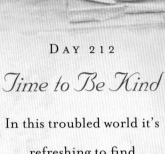

Time to Be Kind

In this troubled world it's

refreshing to find

Someone who still has

the time to be kind.

Always strive to do what is good for

each other and for everyone else.

1 Thessalonians 5:15 niv

How can you be a witness

to the unsaved today?

Walk with Courage

Be glad that you've walked

With courage each day—

Be glad you've had strength

For each step of the way.

Keep steady my steps according to thy promise,
and let no iniquity get dominion over me.

PSALM 119:133

How can you cultivate an atmosphere of
dependence on God in your home?

Happy Memories

Memories are treasures

Time cannot take away,

So may you be surrounded

By happy ones today.

I thank my God every time I remember you.

PHILIPPIANS 1:3 NIV

What treasured memories spring to mind
today? Take the time to thank God for
those joyous times in the past and the
memories you will make tomorrow.

As for Me and My House

What a treasure house filled with rare jewels

Are the blessings of year upon year,

When life has been lived as you've lived it

In a home where God's presence is near.

For through wisdom your days will be many,
and years will be added to your life.

PROVERBS 9:11 NIV

How can you rejoice in
God's presence today?

Journey On

Never give up and never stop—

Just journey on to the mountaintop.

If I have all faith, so as to remove mountains,

but have not love, I am nothing.

1 CORINTHIANS 13:2

How does God provide you with
strength when you are weary?

Ask in Faith

There's no problem too big

And no question too small,

Just ask God in faith

And He'll answer them all.

Commit your work to the LORD,
and your plans will be established.

PROVERBS 16:3

What work have you
committed to the Lord?

DAY 218

Angels All Around

On life's busy thoroughfares

We meet with angels unawares—

Often we're too busy to listen or hear,

Too busy to sense that God is near.

"Truly, I say to you, as you did it not to one
of the least of these, you did it not to me."

MATTHEW 25:45

How do you see God in your
immediate family? At work? At church?

Thanks for the Little Things

Thank You, God, for little things

That often come our way—

The things we take for granted

But don't mention when we pray.

Better is a little with righteousness

than great revenues with injustice.

PROVERBS 16:8

How can you make a conscious
effort to thank God for His
smallest blessings every day?

Tears to Smiles

God is our encouragement

In trouble and in trials,

And in suffering and in sorrow

He will turn our tears to smiles.

May the God of steadfastness
and encouragement grant you to
live in such harmony with one another,
in accord with Christ Jesus.

ROMANS 15:5

Imagine yourself in God's arms.
How is He holding you?

Unexpected Joys

Thank You, God, for little

things that come unexpectedly

To brighten up a dreary day

that dawned so dismally.

It is good to give thanks to the LORD, to sing praises

to thy name, O Most High; to declare thy steadfast

love in the morning, and thy faithfulness by night.

PSALM 92:1–2

How have you experienced an unexpected

joy recently? What can you do to surprise

someone else with a similar blessing?

Warm Our Heart

Oh, God, who made the summer

And warmed the earth with beauty,

Warm our hearts with gratitude

And devotion to our duty.

Enter his gates with thanksgiving, and his courts
with praise! Give thanks to him, bless his name!

PSALM 100:4

What work do you see as a duty?
How can you be thankful for it anyway?

Sunshine and Joy

Thank You, God, for brushing

the dark clouds from my mind

And leaving only sunshine

and joy of heart behind.

Thy testimonies are my heritage for ever;

yea, they are the joy of my heart.

PSALM 119:111

What Bible verse can you plant in your
heart as a shield against loneliness?

Joyous Acceptance

Make us conscious that Your

love comes in many ways

And not always just as happiness

and bright and shining days. . .

Often You send trouble

and we foolishly reject it,

Not realizing that it is Your will

and we should joyously accept it.

He who spares the rod hates his son, but he who

loves him is diligent to discipline him.

PROVERBS 13:24

When has foolishness on your part
been a detriment? How did you
overcome such foolishness?

Strong Faith, True Purpose

Nothing is ever too hard to do

If your faith is strong and

your purpose is true.

But Jesus looked at them and said to them,
"With men this is impossible, but with
God all things are possible."

MATTHEW 19:26

What are the most difficult situations
you are facing? How has your faith
in Christ helped you already?

Mustard Seed Faith

All we really ever need

Is faith as a grain of a mustard seed,

For all God asks is, "Do you believe?"

For if you do ye shall receive.

"For truly, I say to you, if you have faith as a
grain of mustard seed, you will say to this
mountain, 'Move from here to there,' and it will
move; and nothing will be impossible to you."

MATTHEW 17:20

How have you grown spiritually this year?
Are you closer to God or further
away from Him?

Service

Great is our gladness

To serve God through others,

For our Father taught us that

All women are sisters and all men are brothers.

"So whatever you wish that men would do to you,
do so to them; for this is the law and the prophets."

MATTHEW 7:12

Do you know someone who often serves
others? Find a way to serve that person today.

Keep On Believing

Remember, there's no cloud too dark

For God's light to penetrate

If we keep on believing

And have faith enough to wait!

When I sit in darkness,
the LORD will be a light to me.

MICAH 7:8

Do you struggle with anxiety?
How does the Lord provide you with
light and peace during those times?

Bountiful Gifts

More than hearts can imagine

or minds comprehend,

God's bountiful gifts are

ours without end.

The LORD loves righteousness and justice;
the earth is full of his unfailing love.

PSALM 33:5 NIV

When have you been given the gift of a
smile? Of a hug or a kiss? Of a blessing?

Every Good Gift

Thank You, God, for everything—

The big things and the small,

For every good gift comes from God—

The Giver of them all.

For from him and through him and to him
are all things. To him be glory for ever.

ROMANS 11:36

Are you a good gift giver? How does
giving good gifts to others make you feel?
How can you relate this to your
relationship with God?

A Peaceful Isle

God's love is like an island
In life's ocean, vast and wide—
A peaceful, quiet shelter
From the restless, rising tide!

*"I would haste to find me a shelter
from the raging wind and tempest."*

PSALM 55:8

How has God's love and care
brought you peace in the past?

A Sincere Heart

God is always listening to hear

Prayers that are made by a

heart that's sincere.

For everything created by God is good,
and nothing is to be rejected if it is received
with thanksgiving; for then it is consecrated
by the word of God and prayer.

1 TIMOTHY 4:4—5

Which of your friends need
some prayer today?

Hearts and Minds

There's something we should not forget—

That the people we've known,

or heard of, or met

By indirection have had a big part

In molding the thoughts of

the mind and the heart.

A man's mind plans his way,
but the LORD directs his steps.

PROVERBS 16:9

Is there something you've forgiven
but not forgotten? How can you
let go of it today?

He Is Greater

Whatever we ask for

Falls short of God's giving,

For His greatness exceeds

Every facet of living.

Great is the LORD, and greatly to be praised,
and his greatness is unsearchable.

PSALM 145:3

What are your concerns about
monetary matters? How have you
seen God's generosity in the past?

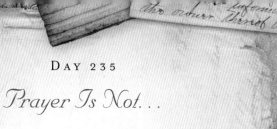

DAY 235

Prayer Is Not...

Prayers are not meant for obtaining

What we selfishly wish to acquire

For God in His wisdom refuses

The things that we wrongly desire.

When I think of thy ordinances from of old,
I take comfort, O LORD.

PSALM 119:52

When has God said no to your prayers
before? When has He said yes?

A Daily Guest

Every home

Is specially blessed

When God becomes

A daily guest.

May God be gracious to us and bless us
and make his face to shine upon us.

PSALM 67:1

What is in your home that
shows visitors your love for God?

Laws to Live By

Let nothing sway you

Or turn you away

From God's old commandments—

They are still new today.

Praise the LORD. Blessed is the man who fears the LORD, who greatly delights in his commandments!

PSALM 112:1

How do you find delight in the laws of the Lord? Are they just a list of rules to you or do they mean more? How did Jesus change the bondage of Old Testament law and how is it still the same?

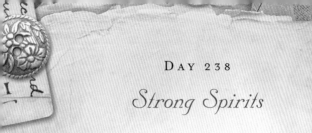

Strong Spirits

Whenever we are troubled

And life has lost its song,

It's God testing us with burdens

Just to make our spirits strong!

*This is my comfort in my affliction
that thy promise gives me life.*

PSALM 119:50

How has God worked through
your times of trial in the past?

DAY 239

Unfailing Medication

When you're feeling downcast,

Seek God in meditation,

For a little talk with Jesus

Is unfailing medication.

I find my delight in thy commandments, which I
love. . . . I will meditate on thy statutes.

PSALM 119:47–48

What steps can you take to change your
negative thoughts to positive ones?

DAY 240

A Meditation Hour

So we may know God better

And feel His quiet power,

Let us daily keep in silence

A meditation hour.

Let the words of my mouth and the meditation
of my heart be acceptable in thy sight,
O LORD, my rock and my redeemer.

PSALM 19:14

What is the best time of day to have
your devotions or quiet time?
How do you feel if you miss a day?

A Baby Is...

A baby is a gift of life

Born of the wonder of love—

A little bit of eternity,

Sent from the Father above.

Lo, sons are a heritage from the LORD,

the fruit of the womb a reward.

PSALM 127:3

How is God's love different
from human love?

Give Joy

Time is not measured

By the years that you live,

But by the deeds that you do

And the joy that you give.

Those who devise good meet
loyalty and faithfulness.

PROVERBS 14:22

What deeds have you done recently
that have given joy to others?

Life Abundant

The more you do unselfishly,

The more you live abundantly. . .

The more of everything you share,

The more you'll always have to spare.

O Lord, my heart is not lifted up, my eyes are not raised too high; I do not occupy myself with things too great and too marvelous for me.

PSALM 131:1

We are mirrors of Christ—
His ambassadors. How does that world
respond to Him through seeing your
actions and deeds?

Think on God

Through a happy springtime

And a summer filled with love

May we walk into the autumn

With our thoughts on God above.

A cheerful heart is a good medicine,
but a downcast spirit dries up the bones.

PROVERBS 17:22

What is your favorite scripture verse?
Why?

Goodness and Mercy

Not money or gifts or material things

But understanding and the joy that it brings

Can change this old world and its selfish ways

And put goodness and mercy back into our days.

*By wisdom a house is built, and by understanding
it is established; by knowledge the rooms are
filled with all precious and pleasant riches.*

PROVERBS 24:3–4

Who is in charge of the finances in your
household? Can you find ways to cut back
and give the money to a needed cause?

DAY 246

God Leads You

Instead of just idle supposing,

Step forward to meet each new day

Secure in the knowledge God's near you

To lead you each step of the way.

When you walk, your step will not be hampered;

and if you run, you will not stumble.

PROVERBS 4:12

Imagine yourself holding God's hand.

Where is He leading you?

Bundled Troubles

Whenever I am troubled

And lost in deep despair,

I bundle all my troubles up

And go to God in prayer.

He will regard the prayer of the destitute,
and will not despise their supplication.

PSALM 102:17

Why is it so difficult to wait for
God's answers—or to wait at all?

A Haven of Love

God's love is like a beacon

Burning bright with faith and prayer,

And through the changing scenes of life

We can find a haven there!

Then they were glad because they had quiet,
and he brought them to their desired haven.

PSALM 107:30

What Bible verse can you set in your
heart as a shield against worry?

God's Preference

When someone does a kindness,

It always seems to me

That's the way God up in heaven

Would like us all to be.

Teach me thy way, O LORD, that I may walk
in thy truth; unite my heart to fear thy name.

PSALM 86:11

In what ways can you demonstrate
kindness to others or to yourself?

Withdraw in Prayer

When life becomes a problem

Much too great for you to bear,

Instead of trying to escape,

Just withdraw in prayer.

Many are the afflictions of the righteous;
but the LORD delivers him out of them all.

PSALM 34:19

In prayer, do you approach God
reverently or casually? Is this how
you think of and treat God also?
Do you need to make a change?

Gifts from the Heart

With our hands we give gifts

that money cannot buy.

Diamonds that sparkle

like stars in the sky,

But only the heart can give away

The gift of peace and a perfect day.

May the LORD give strength to his people!
May the LORD bless his people with peace!

PSALM 29:11

Can you describe the difference between
the peace of God and peace with God?

Lovely Miracles

God sends His little angels

In many forms and guises,

They come as lovely miracles

That God alone devises.

Thy hands have made and fashioned me;
give me understanding that I may
learn thy commandments.

PSALM 119:73

What can you learn from people
who are different from you?
What characteristics do you see in them?

I Need Peace

"Thou wilt keep him in perfect peace

Whose mind is stayed on thee."

And, God, if anyone needs peace,

It certainly is me!

A man's spirit will endure sickness;
but a broken spirit who can bear?

PROVERBS 18:14

Do you need to get rid of some
bitterness in your life right now?

God Loves You Still

Somebody cares and always will,

The world forgets but God loves you still.

You cannot go beyond His love

No matter what you're guilty of.

For thou, O Lord, art good and forgiving,
abounding in steadfast love to all who call on thee.

PSALM 86:5

Do you struggle with guilt? Do you need to
ask for the Lord's forgiveness, or is Satan
simply using this feeling to keep you down?

DAY 255

He Never Forsakes

The seasons swiftly come and go

and with them comes the thought

Of all the various changes that

time in its flight has brought,

But one thing never changes,

it remains the same forever,

God truly loves His children

and He will forsake them never!

Hide not thy face from me. Turn not thy servant
away in anger, thou who hast been my help.
Cast me not off, forsake me not, O God of my salvation!

PSALM 27:9

What are some of the ways
God shows His love for us?

A Rich Reward

The love you give to others

Is returned to you by the Lord. . .

And the love of God

Is your soul's rich reward.

One man gives freely, yet grows all the richer;
another withholds what he should give,
and only suffers want.

PROVERBS 11:24

How can you cultivate an
atmosphere of love in your home?

Tender Memories

Tender little memories

Of some word or deed

Give us strength and courage

When we are in need.

The righteous will never be moved;
he will be remembered for ever.

PSALM 112:6

When have someone's words encouraged
you? What did he or she say?

The Father's Protection

Remember God loves you

And wants to protect you,

So seek that small haven

And be guided by prayer

To that place of protection

Within God's loving care.

Every word of God is flawless;
he is a shield to those who take refuge in him.

PROVERBS 30:5 NIV

When do you need a safe place to rest?

Morning, Noon, and Night

Meet God in the morning

And go with Him through the day

And thank Him for His guidance

Each evening when you pray.

O LORD, in the morning thou dost hear my voice;
in the morning I prepare a sacrifice for thee, and watch.

PSALM 5:3

How has God guided your life so far?

Patience and Contentment

Teach me to be patient

In everything I do,

Content to trust Your wisdom

And to follow after You.

Fret not yourself because of evildoers, and be not
envious of the wicked; for the evil man has no
future; the lamp of the wicked will be put out.

PROVERBS 24:19–20

Are you content with God, your husband,
your children, your home, your job?
In what areas are you discontent?

Higher Goals

Father up in heaven,

Stir and wake our sleeping souls,

Renew our faith and lift us up

And give us higher goals.

*I press on toward the goal to win the
prize for which God has called me
heavenward in Christ Jesus.*

PHILIPPIANS 3:14 NIV

What are some of your goals
for the next five years?

Show Love to All

To be peaceful, I must be kind

For peace can't exist in a hate-torn mind,

So to have peace I must always show

Love to all people I meet, see, or know.

He who respects the
commandment will be rewarded.

PROVERBS 13:13

What steals joy and peace from your
heart? How can you combat these issues?

Worship Everywhere

I have worshipped in churches

and chapels,

I have prayed in the busy street,

I have sought my God and

have found Him

Where the waves of the ocean beat.

O come, let us worship and bow down,
let us kneel before the LORD, our Maker!

PSALM 95:6

Think of a time in your life when
God seemed intimately close to you.
Do you feel the same way today?

Peace of Soul

Only by the grace of God

Can we gain self-control,

And only meditative thoughts

Can restore our peace of soul.

In peace I will both lie down and sleep;
for thou alone, O LORD, makest me dwell in safety.

PSALM 4:8

In what past situations should
you have prayed for self-control?

God's Goodness Prevails

Wait with a heart that is patient
For the goodness of God to prevail,
For never do our prayers go unanswered,
And His mercy and love never fail.

Be still before the LORD,
and wait patiently for him.

PSALM 37:7

Do you ever feel that your prayers go
unanswered? How do you feel when
others' prayers are answered?

It's a Wonderful World

God is so lavish in all that He's done

To make this great world

such a wonderful one. . .

His mountains are high,

His oceans are deep,

And vast and unmeasured

the prairielands sweep.

In his hand are the depths of the earth;
the heights of the mountains are his also.

PSALM 95:4

What part of God's creation
do you find most amazing?

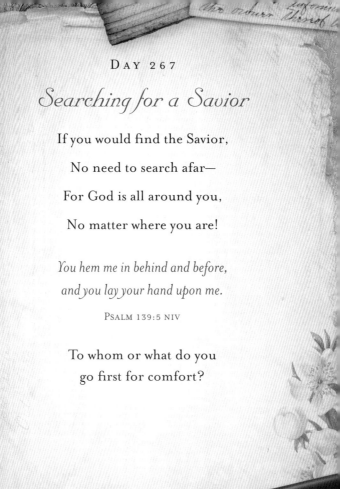

Searching for a Savior

If you would find the Savior,

No need to search afar—

For God is all around you,

No matter where you are!

You hem me in behind and before,
and you lay your hand upon me.

PSALM 139:5 NIV

To whom or what do you
go first for comfort?

Replenish My Soul

It fills me with joy just to linger with You

As my soul You replenish

and my heart You renew,

For prayer is much more

than just asking for things—

It's the peace and contentment

that quietness brings.

The LORD, your God, is in your midst. . .
he will rejoice over you with gladness,
he will renew you in his love.

ZEPHANIAH 3:17

When are you most content?

My Loved Ones

Father, hear this little prayer—

Reach across the miles from here to there,

So I can feel much closer to

those I'm fondest of,

And they may know I think of them

with thankfulness and love.

"Hear my prayer, O LORD, and give ear to my cry;
hold not thy peace at my tears! For I am thy
passing guest, a sojourner, like all my fathers."

PSALM 39:12

How often do you pray for your family
and friends who live far away? How do
you pray for them? How can you reach
out and let them know you care?

Infinite Sky

Each day at dawning

I lift my heart high

And raise up my eyes

To the infinite sky.

*You will do well to pay attention to this as to a
lamp shining in a dark place, until the day dawns
and the morning star rises in your hearts.*

2 PETER 1:19

How are you at giving thanks when trials
come? Can you give thanks for specifics
in the situation even if you aren't happy
about the situation in general?

More Equals Less

The more you give,

The more you get—

The more you laugh,

The less you fret!

The meek shall possess the land,
and delight themselves in abundant prosperity.

PSALM 37:11

What Bible verse can you set in your
heart as a shield against criticism?

Shine

Do not sit and idly wish for wider,

new dimensions

Where you can put in practice

your good intentions,

But at the spot God placed you,

begin at once to do

Little things to brighten up

the lives surrounding you.

The path of the righteous is like the light of dawn,
which shines brighter and brighter until full day.

PROVERBS 4:18

Are you following God's will and
what He wants you to be doing?

The Unknown

The future is not ours to know,

And it may never be—

So let us live and give our best,

And give it lavishly.

Let not your heart envy sinners, but continue in
the fear of the LORD all the day. Surely there is a
future, and your hope will not be cut off.

PROVERBS 23:17—18

Are you looking at the future with
eyes of faith or with eyes of fear?

God Is beside You

Always remember

That whatever betide you,

You are never alone

For God is beside you.

God is our refuge and strength,
a very present help in trouble.

PSALM 46:1

Has someone betrayed you?
How did you feel, then and now?
Have you ever betrayed a friend?

He's in Control

Humbly, I realize

That He who made the sea and skies

And holds the whole world in His hand

Also has my small soul in His command.

The law of the LORD is perfect,
reviving the soul. . .the commandment of the
LORD is pure, enlightening the eyes.

PSALM 19:7–8

In what areas do you find it
difficult to give up control?

Let God Talk

When your day is pressure-packed

And your hours are all too few,

Just close your eyes and meditate

And let God talk to you.

May my meditation be pleasing to him,
for I rejoice in the LORD.

PSALM 104:34

Are you currently in a stressful time?
Can you turn the situation over to God?
If you've already done so, what measure
of peace have you found since?

Stepping-Stones

Welcome every stumbling block

And every thorn and jagged rock,

For each one is a stepping-stone

To God who wants you for His own.

He drew me up from the desolate pit,
out of the miry bog, and set my feet upon
a rock, making my steps secure.

PSALM 40:2

How can you show your obedience to
God? Why do people often disobey Him?

The Power of Faith

Faith is a force that is greater

Than knowledge or power or skill,

And the darkest defeat turns to triumph

If we trust in God's wisdom and will.

Trust in the LORD, and do good; so you will
dwell in the land, and enjoy security. . . .
Commit your way to the LORD; trust in him,
and he will act.

PSALM 37:3, 5

When—or why—do you find it difficult
to trust God? Is it easier to trust Him
in the big things or the little things?

God's Help

Only with the help of God

Can we meet the vast unknown. . .

Even the strongest cannot

Do the job alone!

Be pleased, O God, to deliver me!
O LORD, make haste to help me!

PSALM 70:1

Who in your life is a woman of courage,
like Deborah or Esther? Why did you
choose this particular woman?

Rejoice in Adversity

The way we use adversity

Is strictly our own choice,

For in God's hands adversity

Can make the heart rejoice.

I will rejoice and be glad for thy steadfast love,

because thou hast seen my affliction,

thou hast taken heed of my adversities.

PSALM 31:7

When has your heart rejoiced during
adversity because of God?

Simple Faith

Father, grant once more to men

A simple, childlike faith again,

Forgetting color, race, or creed

And seeing only the heart's deep need.

Faith is the assurance of things hoped for,
the conviction of things not seen.

HEBREWS 11:1

Have you totally surrendered your life
to Christ? If not, what is keeping you
from doing so? Do you daily surrender
your days to Him?

Let Him Lead You

Take the Savior's loving hand

And do not try to understand,

Just let Him lead you where He will

Through pastures green, by waters still.

Know that the LORD is God! It is he that made us,
and we are his; we are his people,
and the sheep of his pasture.

PSALM 100:3

How has God ministered
to you in a hard place?

A Cup of Kindness

Take a cup of kindness,

Mix it well with love,

Add a lot of patience

And faith in God above.

With patience a ruler may be persuaded,
and a soft tongue will break a bone.

PROVERBS 25:15

If you were to ask God to give
you one fruit of the Spirit,
what would it be and why?

New Friends

May we try

In our small way

To make new friends

From day to day.

A faithful envoy brings healing.

PROVERBS 13:17

How can you be a friend today to someone who needs love or a kind word?

Words Unspoken

Prayer is so often just words unspoken,

Whispered in tears by a heart that is broken,

For God is already deeply aware

Of the burdens we find too heavy to bear.

I am utterly spent and crushed;
I groan because of the tumult of my heart.

PSALM 38:8

When was the last time you were broken
before God, confessing sin and asking for
repentance? Do you need to do so again?

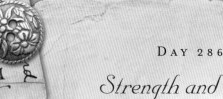

Strength and Cheer

God's kindness is ever around you,

Always ready to freely impart

Strength to your faltering spirit,

Cheer to your lonely heart.

When the cares of my heart are many,

thy consolations cheer my soul.

PSALM 94:19

How can you praise God today for the
works He has done in your life lately?

Life's Autumn

What a wonderful time is life's autumn,

When the leaves of the trees are all gold,

When God fills each day as He sends it

With memories priceless and old.

One man esteems one day as better than another,
while another man esteems all days alike.

ROMANS 14:5

What memories has God blessed you
with that you prize above others?

Deeper Beauty

Discipline in daily duty

Will shape your life for deeper beauty,

And as you grow in strength and grace,

The more clearly you can see God's face.

May God be gracious to us and bless us
and make his face to shine upon us.

PSALM 67:1

Do you struggle with gossip?
How can you take an active role in
guarding your mouth from this sin?

DAY 289

God Is Real

What better answers are there

To prove God's holy being

Than the wonders all around us

That are ours just for the seeing.

"Stop and consider the wondrous works of God."

JOB 37:14

What things in nature give you great joy?
A tiny hummingbird, a majestic
mountain, the changing of the seasons,
the wind on your face, the beauty
of pristine snow?

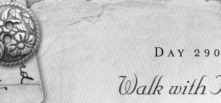

Walk with Him

May you walk with Him

And dwell in His love

As He sends you good gifts

From heaven above.

Walk in love, as Christ loved us
and gave himself up for us.

EPHESIANS 5:2

What is the difference between
a "want" and a "need"?

Real Contentment

It's by completing

What God gives us to do

That we find real contentment

And happiness, too.

Requite them according to their work,

and according to the evil of their deeds;

requite them according to the work of

their hands; render them their due reward.

PSALM 28:4

What jobs do you find

satisfaction in doing?

The Importance of Prayer

Whenever you are hurried

And must leave something undone,

Be sure it's not your prayer to God

At dawn or setting sun.

It is good to give thanks to the LORD,
to sing praises to thy name, O Most High;
to declare thy steadfast love in the morning,
and thy faithfulness by night.

PSALM 92:1–2

Imagine yourself at God's feet.
What is He saying to you?

A Cheerful Song

I sometimes think that friendliness

Is something like a cheerful song. . .

It makes the good days better,

And it helps when things go wrong.

The LORD is my strength and my shield; in him my
heart trusts; so I am helped, and my heart exults,
and with my song I give thanks to him.

PSALM 28:7

What have you learned
from a friend this week?

Nighttime Prayers

I meet God in the morning

And go with Him through the day,

Then in the stillness of the night

Before sleep comes, I pray.

I rise before dawn and cry for help; I hope in thy words. My eyes are awake before the watches of the night, that I may meditate upon thy promise.

PSALM 119:147–148

Are you guilty of neglecting your prayer life? How can you change that this week?

A New Day

See the dew glisten as a new day is born,

Hear the birds sing on the wings

of the morn.

From the rising of the sun to its setting

the name of the LORD is to be praised!

PSALM 113:3

Do you like to hear the birds sing?

What are your thoughts when you

hear them in the morning?

The Temple of God

The house of prayer is no farther away

Than the quiet spot where you kneel and pray,

For the heart is a temple when God is there

As you place yourself in His loving care.

I bow down toward thy holy temple and give thanks to
thy name for thy steadfast love and thy faithfulness;
for thou hast exalted above everything thy name and thy word.

PSALM 138:2

When has God come to your rescue?

Keep Climbing

Faith is a mover of mountains,

And there's nothing that God cannot do,

So start out today with faith in your heart

And climb till your dream comes true!

LORD, *thou hast been our dwelling place in all*
generations. Before the mountains were brought
forth, or ever thou hadst formed the earth and the
world, from everlasting to everlasting thou art God.

PSALM 90:1–2

What are you believing by faith
that the Lord will do for you?

A Fortress of Faith

Be not disheartened by troubles,

For trials are the building blocks

On which to erect a fortress of faith

Secure on God's ageless rocks.

In thee, O LORD, do I take refuge;

let me never be put to shame! . . .

Be thou to me a rock of refuge,

a strong fortress, to save me,

for thou art my rock and my fortress.

PSALM 71:1, 3

What Bible verse can you set in
your heart as a shield against fear?

The Blessings of Friendship

Father, make us kind and wise

So we may always recognize

The blessings that are ours to take

And the friendships that are ours to make.

There are friends who pretend to be friends,
but there is a friend who sticks closer than a brother.

PROVERBS 18:24

How can you grow in wisdom?

A Happy Heart

Cheerful thoughts like sunbeams

Lighten up the darkest fears,

For when the heart is happy

There's just no time for tears.

A glad heart makes a cheerful countenance,
but by sorrow of heart the spirit is broken.

PROVERBS 15:13

Do you have a grateful spirit—
toward your job, your family,
your home, and others?

Walk Humbly

Do justice, love kindness,

walk humbly with God. . .

All things worth having

are yours to achieve

If you follow God's words

and have faith to believe!

He loves righteousness and justice;
the earth is full of the steadfast love of the LORD.

PSALM 33:5

Can you list ten of your good qualities
and five of your weaknesses? Read aloud
the list of your good qualities, and give
God your weaknesses.

The Needed Spark

An unlit candle gives no light—

Only when burning is it shining bright;

And if life is empty, dull, and dark,

It's doing things for others

that gives the needed spark.

Yea, thou dost light my lamp;
the LORD my God lightens my darkness.

PSALM 18:28

How can you bless your minister or
your minister's spouse this week?

Bitter and Sweet

Everything is by comparison

Both the bitter and the sweet,

And it takes a bit of both of them

To make our lives complete.

He who is sated loathes honey, but to one

who is hungry everything bitter is sweet.

PROVERBS 27:7

What things in your life are "bitter"?
What things are "sweet"? How can you
learn to appreciate both?

Loving Hearts

Some folks grow older

with birthdays, it's true,

But others grow nicer

as years widen their view.

No one will notice a few little wrinkles

When a kind, loving heart fills

the eyes full of twinkles.

Grandchildren are the crown of the aged.

PROVERBS 17:6

How do you feel you are aging?
Are you growing nicer as the years go by?

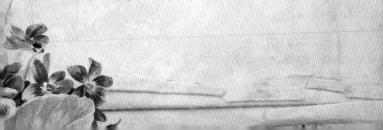

The Master Plan

All things work together

To complete the master plan,

And God up in heaven

Can see what's best for man.

Yet God my King is from of old,
working salvation in the midst of the earth.

PSALM 74:12

What do you do when a
cherished dream falls apart?

Everything Is His

Someday may man realize

That all the earth, the seas, and skies

Belong to God, who made us all,

The rich, the poor, the great, the small.

Who has ascended to heaven and come down?
Who has gathered the wind in his fists?
Who has wrapped up the waters in a garment?
Who has established all the ends of the earth?
What is his name, and what is his son's name?
Surely you know!

PROVERBS 30:4

How do you acquire inspiration?
Think about a time that you were
overwhelmed by God's greatness.
What effect did that have on you?

Patience and Grace

God, give us patience and grace to endure

And a stronger faith so we feel secure

And instead of remembering,

help up forget

The irritations that caused us to fret.

Therefore, as God's chosen people,
holy and dearly loved, clothe yourselves
with compassion, kindness, humility,
gentleness and patience.

COLOSSIANS 3:12 NIV

Do you catch yourself complaining
or find yourself easily irritated?
How can you work on these attitudes
to show a more Christlike one?

Grow in the Hard Times

Trouble is part and parcel of life,

And no man can grow without

trouble and strife,

And the steep hills ahead and

the high mountain peaks

Afford man at last the peace that he seeks.

"You will go out in joy and be led forth in peace;
the mountains and hills will burst into song before you,
and all the trees of the field will clap their hands."

ISAIAH 55:12 NIV

Has peace come at a high cost to you?
Are you still looking for peace? How is God
helping you through these challenges?

Kindness Matters

A warm, ready smile or a kind,

thoughtful deed

Or a hand outstretched

in an hour of need

Can change our outlook

and make the world bright

Where a minute before just

nothing seemed right.

A brother helped is like a strong city,
but quarreling is like the bars of a castle.

When has a smile meant a great
deal to you? When have you helped
someone by offering a smile?

Kindred Hearts

The golden chain of friendship

Is a strong and blessed tie

Binding kindred hearts together

As the years go passing by.

Do good, O LORD, to those who are good,
and to those who are upright in their hearts!

PSALM 125:4

What fond remembrances do you have of
times with friends or family? What are those
links that bound you together in love?

DAY 311

A Gentle Heart

God in His loving and all-wise way

Makes the heart that was young one day

Serene and more gentle

and less restless, too,

Content to remember the

joys it once knew.

Remember, LORD, your great mercy and love,
for they are from of old.

PSALM 25:6 NIV

Why does God say women who have a
gentle and quiet spirit are of great worth
to God (1 Peter 3:3–5)? How do you
rank, on a scale of 1 to 10?

Heartfelt Conversation

Take ample time

For heartfelt conversation,

Establish with our Father

An unbreakable relation.

A word fitly spoken is like apples
of gold in a setting of silver.

PROVERBS 25:11

We are told to "pray constantly"
(1 Thessalonians 5:17). Do you find
this instruction to be a challenge?
Are you striving toward this goal?

A Perfect Plan

God does nothing without purpose—
Everything's a perfect plan
To fulfill in bounteous measure
All He has ever promised man.

Cast your cares on the LORD
and he will sustain you.

PSALM 55:22 NIV

What promises has God already
fulfilled for you or in you?

Gifts All Around

Every happy happening

And every lucky break

Are little gifts from God above

That are ours to freely take.

The steps of a man are from the LORD,
and he establishes him in whose way he delights.

PSALM 37:23

Has God provided for all your needs?
Has He provided for some of your wants?

The Heart's Haven

Help all people everywhere

who must often dwell apart

To know that they're together

in the haven of the heart.

If we love one another,
God abides in us and his love is perfected in us.

1 JOHN 4:12

If your house caught fire, what would
you save first? What unused or
unnecessary things in your home
can you give away to others?

No More Cares

I pray that God will just take over

All the problems I couldn't solve,

And I'm ready for tomorrow

With all my cares dissolved.

Even the sparrow finds a home, and the swallow
a nest for herself, where she may lay her young,
at thy altars, O LORD of hosts, my King and my God.

PSALM 84:3

List two things you worry about the most.
How can you overcome a habit of worry and
place your trust in God for these things?

Growing Older

Growing older only means
The spirit grows serene,
And we behold things with our souls
That our eyes have never seen.

Even to old age and gray hairs, O God,
do not forsake me, till I proclaim thy might
to all the generations to come.

PSALM 71:18

How do the examples of biblical men and
women inspire and encourage you?

The Virtue of Kindness

Kindness is a virtue

Given by the Lord,

It pays dividends in happiness

And joy is its reward.

A wicked man earns deceptive wages,
but one who sows righteousness gets a sure reward.

PROVERBS 11:18

When has doing something for others
made you happy? What have you
done for those less fortunate?

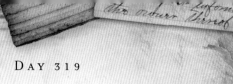

A Thankful Heart

The joy of enjoying

And the fullness of living

Are found in the heart

That is filled with thanksgiving.

Deceit is in the heart of those who devise evil,
but those who plan good have joy.

PROVERBS 12:20

How can you cultivate an
atmosphere of joy in your home?

Wonderful World

It's a wonderful world and it always will be

If we keep our eyes open and focused to see

The wonderful things man is capable of

When he opens his heart to

God and His love.

God looks down from heaven upon
the sons of men to see if there are any
that are wise, that seek after God.

PSALM 53:2

Where do you see God best reflected in
humankind? How can you encourage
others to continue to do the "wonderful
things" they are capable of, instead
of giving in to a sinful nature?

Creative God

In the beauty of a snowflake,

Falling softly on the land,

Is the mystery and miracle

Of God's great, creative hand!

Praise the LORD from the earth, . . .
fire and hail, snow and frost, stormy
wind fulfilling his command!

PSALM 148:7–8

How is the world better because we are as
individualistic as the snowflakes?

All God Asks

It's hard to believe

That God asks no more

Than to bring Him our problems

And then close the door.

The LORD is a stronghold for the oppressed,
a stronghold in times of trouble. And those who
know thy name put their trust in thee, for thou,
O LORD, hast not forsaken those who seek thee.

PSALM 9:9–10

Do you find yourself speaking negatively
about your husband or children?
How are you reminded to focus
on their positive qualities?

My Prayer for Today

I give to You my thanks

And my heart kneels to pray—

God keep me and guide me

And go with me today.

Thou dost guide me with thy counsel,
and afterward thou wilt receive me to glory.

PSALM 73:24

How have you seen God guide
you in your everyday life?

The Key to Living

Help us to remember

That the key to life and living

Is to make each prayer a prayer of thanks

And every day "Thanksgiving."

I will praise the name of God with a song;
I will magnify him with thanksgiving.

PSALM 69:30

What talents or gifts did God
instill in you? How are you using
these gifts to help others?

Real Thanksgiving

Dear God, no words are great enough

to thank You for just living,

And that is why every day is

a day for real thanksgiving.

Let us come into his presence with thanksgiving;

let us make a joyful noise to him with songs of praise!

PSALM 95:2

Have you thanked God today for

the lives of your family and those

who are close to you?

Uncounted Jewels

God's heavens are dotted

with uncounted jewels,

For joy without measure

is one of God's rules,

His hand is so generous,

His heart is so great,

He comes not too soon,

and He comes not too late.

Of old thou didst lay the foundation of the earth,
and the heavens are the work of thy hands.

PSALM 102:25

Whom haven't you seen in a while?
Pray a prayer of blessing for that person.

Endless Supply

God, I know that I love You,

And I know without doubt

That Your goodness and mercy

Never run out.

Have mercy on me, O God, according to
thy steadfast love; according to thy abundant
mercy blot out my transgressions.

PSALM 51:1

How can you extend God's goodness
and mercy to others this week?

DAY 328

The Earth Is His

"The earth is the Lord's
And the fullness thereof"—
It speaks of His greatness,
It sings of His love.

The heavens are thine, the earth also is thine;
the world and all that is in it, thou hast founded them.

PSALM 89:11

How would you describe
the Lord Almighty?

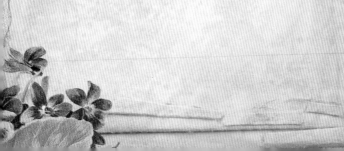

Stop and Pray

Do you pause in meditation

Upon life's thoroughfare,

And offer up thanksgiving—

Or say a word of prayer?

I revere thy commandments, which I love,
and I will meditate on thy statutes.

PSALM 119:48

How do you consciously take the time to
be still in your daily schedule? Is there
anything you need cut out to allow for
more time in meditation?

Sweet Forbearance

Teach me sweet forbearance

When things do not go right,

So I remain unruffled

When others grow uptight.

If you faint in the day of adversity,
your strength is small.

PROVERBS 24:10

What Bible verse can you set in
your heart when you need patience?

Day 331

Joy Every Step

Prayers are the stairs that lead to God,

And there's joy every step of the way

When we make our pilgrimage to Him

With love in our hearts each day.

The steps of a man are from the LORD,
and he establishes him in whose way he delights.

PSALM 37:23

Do you need to take time to
rest and recharge today?

A Quiet Heart

Teach me how to quiet

My racing, rising heart

So I may hear the answer

You are trying to impart.

My son, give me your heart,
and let your eyes observe my ways.

PROVERBS 23:26

Do you ever assume what God's answers are
going to be to your petitions without really
taking the time to listen? What happens
when your assumptions are incorrect?

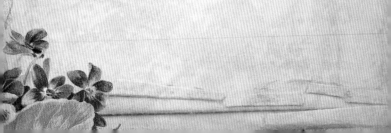

Give and Give and Give Again

Only what we give away

Enriches us from day to day.

*He who sows sparingly will also reap sparingly,
and he who sows bountifully will also reap bountifully.*

2 CORINTHIANS 9:6

When have you given more than you
thought you could? What kind of blessings
did you experience in return?

DAY 334

He Understands

Whenever you are troubled,

Put your problems in God's hand,

For He has faced all problems,

And He will understand.

*"Glory to God in the highest heaven, and on earth
peace to those on whom his favor rests."*

LUKE 2:14 NIV

Do you ever doubt the Lord's love
for you? How has God spoken the
truth to you in the past to help you
overcome these doubts?

God's Loving Care

Place yourself in God's loving care,

And He will gladly help you bear

Whatever lies ahead of you,

And He will see you safely through.

"Behold, God is my salvation; I will trust,
and will not be afraid; for the LORD GOD is my
strength and my song, and he has become my salvation."

ISAIAH 12:2

What times of challenge or rejoicing
are forthcoming in your life?
Ask God to prepare you for each.

The Best of Days

With a sweet nostalgia we longingly recall

The happy days of long ago

that seem the best of all.

I have been young, and now am old.

PSALM 37:25

What are some of your favorite holiday
memories you've made with your family?
What new traditions can you incorporate
to make new memories?

My Comforter

Oh, God, what a comfort

To know that You care

And to know when I seek You,

You will always be there!

"As for me, I would seek God,
and to God would I commit my cause."

JOB 5:8

Why is mercy important? When in your
life have you been shown mercy?

His Holy Birth

The holy Christ Child came

down to live on earth,

And that is why we celebrate His holy,

wondrous birth.

*"For to you is born this day in the city of
David a Savior, who is Christ the Lord."*

LUKE 2:11

Which biblical story means the
most to you? What Bible character
can you relate to the most?

God's Divine Gift

What is love? No words can define it.

It's something so great,

only God could design it.

Yes, love is beyond what man can define,

For love is immortal and

God's gift divine.

To him who alone does great wonders,
for his steadfast love endures for ever.

PSALM 136:4

What is the best gift you've ever received?
What is the best gift you've ever given?

Open the Door

We open the door to let joy walk through

When we learn to expect

the best and most, too,

For believing we'll find a happy surprise

Makes reality out of a fancied surmise!

May the God of hope fill you with all joy
and peace in believing, so that by the power
of the Holy Spirit you may abound in hope.

ROMANS 15:13

What has been your happiest
surprise in your life so far?

A Loving Heart

Remember, a kind and thoughtful deed

Or a hand outstretched in time of need

Is the rarest of gifts, for it is a part

Not of the purse, but a loving heart.

Little children, let us not love in word
or speech but in deed and in truth.

1 JOHN 3:18

What intangible gifts have meant
the most to you and why?

God's Face

The silent stars in timeless skies,

The wonderment in children's eyes,

A rosebud in a slender vase

Are all reflections of God's face.

Hear, O LORD, when I cry aloud, be gracious to
me and answer me! Thou hast said, "Seek ye my
face." My heart says to thee, "Thy face, LORD,
do I seek." Hide not thy face from me.

PSALM 27:7–9

What have you learned about God
and the world through children?

Peace and Goodwill

We pray to Thee, our Father,

As Christmas comes again,

For peace among all nations

And goodwill between all men.

*"Whatever house you enter, first say,
'Peace be to this house!'"*

LUKE 10:5

Though it may not be on an international
scale, how can you promote goodwill
where you are?

Only Jesus

Only through the Christ Child

can man be born again,

For God sent the baby Jesus

as the Savior of all men.

This is how the birth of Jesus the Messiah came

about: His mother Mary was pledged to be

married to Joseph, but before they came together,

she was found to be pregnant through the Holy Spirit.

MATTHEW 1:18 NIV

When you picture Jesus as a tiny baby,

what are your feelings and thoughts?

No Reason at All

In counting our blessings,

We find when we're through

We've no reason at all

To complain or be blue.

A faithful man will abound with blessings.

PROVERBS 28:20

For what reason, characteristic,
personality trait, or act of kindness
do you wish to be remembered?

The First Christmas

May the holy remembrance

Of the first Christmas Day

Be our reassurance

Christ is not far away.

Upon thee was I cast from my birth, and since my
mother bore me thou hast been my God.

PSALM 22:10

What can you do to brighten your
coworker's or neighbor's day?

Good Cheer

May every heart and every home
Continue through the year
To feel the warmth and wonderment
Of this season of good cheer.

The unfolding of thy words gives light;
it imparts understanding to the simple.

PSALM 119:130

What is your favorite Christmas
tradition? Why is it special to you?

Eternal Glory

Make us aware

That the Christmas story

Is everyone's promise

Of eternal glory.

Not to us, O LORD, not to us, but to thy
name give glory, for the sake of thy
steadfast love and thy faithfulness!

PSALM 115:1

What can you do to give love away today—
without buying, boxing, wrapping, or
tying? How can you show that God is love?

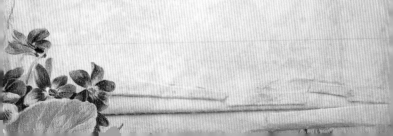

A Better Place

The priceless gift of life is love,

For with the help of God above,

Love can change the human race

And make this world a better place.

This is the message you heard from the beginning:
We should love one another.

1 JOHN 3:11 NIV

What can you do to uplift the frazzled
salesclerks and others around you?

Unselfish Giving

If we lived Christmas each

day as we should,

And made it our aim to always do good,

We'd find the lost key to

meaningful living

That comes not from getting,

but from unselfish giving.

He is ever giving liberally and lending,
and his children become a blessing.

PSALM 37:26

What is the difference between
happiness and joy?

New Hope

Just like the seasons that come and go

When the flowers of spring

lie buried in snow,

God sends to the heart

in its winter of sadness

A springtime awakening of

new hope and gladness.

"And now, Lord, for what do I wait?
My hope is in thee."

PSALM 39:7

What daily occurrences give you hope?
How can you share this hope with
someone who needs it?

The Christmas Star

It matters not who or what you are;

All men can behold the Christmas Star.

For the Star that shone is shining still

In the hearts of men of peace and goodwill.

Cast me not away from thy presence, and take not thy holy Spirit from me. Restore to me the joy of thy salvation, and uphold me with a willing spirit.

PSALM 51:11—12

How can you show not only the Christmas spirit but the Christian spirit to those with whom you come in contact this month?

Glad Tidings

In the glad tidings

Of the first Christmas night,

God showed us

The way and the truth and the light.

Oh send out thy light and thy truth;
let them lead me, let them bring me to
thy holy hill and to thy dwelling!

PSALM 43:3

How can you show others the
way in truth and light today?

DAY 354

Heart Awakening

Give us faith to believe again

That peace on earth, goodwill to men

Will follow this winter of man's mind

And awaken his heart and make him kind.

And let us not grow weary in well-doing,
for in due season we shall reap, if we do not lose heart.

GALATIANS 6:9

Does your heart need awakening today?
Ask Jesus to give you a spiritual awakening.

Humble Christ Child

God, make us aware that in Thy name

The holy Christ child humbly came

To live on earth and leave behind

New faith and hope for all mankind.

I wait for the LORD, my soul waits,
and in his word I hope.

PSALM 130:5

Imagine being one of the magi.
What would you have said to the baby
Jesus when you first met Him?

The Christmas Pattern

The gifts that we give have no purpose

Unless God is part of the giving,

And unless we make Christmas a pattern

To be followed in everyday living.

A man's gift makes room for him
and brings him before great men.

PROVERBS 18:16

What characteristics of Christmas
can you adopt throughout the year?

Salvation

Christmas to me

Is a gift from above—

A gift of salvation

Born of God's love.

Steadfast love and faithfulness will meet;
righteousness and peace will kiss each other.

PSALM 85:10

What does Christmas mean to you?

More Than a Season

Christmas is more than a

day at the end of the year,

More than a season of

joy and good cheer,

Christmas is really God's

pattern for living

To be followed all year

by unselfish giving.

I give thee thanks, O LORD, with my whole heart.

PSALM 138:1

Do you make it a habit to give all
year long? To whom do you give?
What causes are closest to your heart?

Infinite Living

Christmas is more

Than getting and giving—

It's the why and the wherefore

Of infinite living.

*"Therefore I command you, You shall
open wide your hand to your brother,
to the needy and to the poor, in the land."*

DEUTERONOMY 15:11

Can you help at a homeless shelter
or soup kitchen or donate to a
food bank this month?

The Miracle of Christmas

Miracles are marvels

That defy all explanation,

And Christmas is a miracle

And not just a celebration.

I will give to the LORD the thanks due to
his righteousness, and I will sing praise to
the name of the LORD, the Most High.

PSALM 7:17

When have you witnessed or heard of a
modern-day miracle? What was it?

DAY 361

Keep Christ in Christmas

By keeping Christ in Christmas

We are helping to fulfill

The glad tidings of the angels—

"Peace on earth and to men, goodwill."

Let me hear what God the LORD will speak,
for he will speak peace to his people, to his saints,
to those who turn to him in their hearts.

PSALM 85:8

How do you keep Christ in Christmas?
How can you encourage others
to do the same?

Common Ground

Peace on earth cannot be found

Until we meet on common ground

And every man becomes a brother

Who worships God and loves all others.

Beloved, if God so loved us,
we also ought to love one another.

1 JOHN 4:11

Do you consider your love for your
brothers and sisters to be a form
of worship? Why or why not?

DAY 363

Every Good Gift

The richest gifts are God's to give,

May you possess them as long as you live.

Every good endowment and every perfect gift is from
above, coming down from the Father of lights with
whom there is no variation or shadow due to change.

JAMES 1:17

What are some of God's richest gifts?
Which of these have you received?

Listen

Above the noise and laughter

That is empty, cruel, and loud,

Do you listen for the voice of God

In the restless surging crowd?

God is our refuge and strength,
a very present help in trouble.

PSALM 46:1

Does God have to get your attention
with a deafening noise—
or can He do it with a whisper?

Year-End Blessings

Thank You, dear God,

for the year that now ends

And for the great blessing

of loved ones and friends.

Thou crownest the year with thy bounty.

PSALM 65:11

What has God taught you

about yourself this year?

What have you learned about Him?

Scripture Index

OLD TESTAMENT

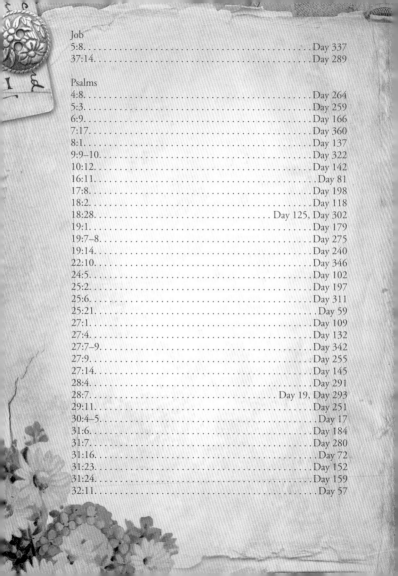

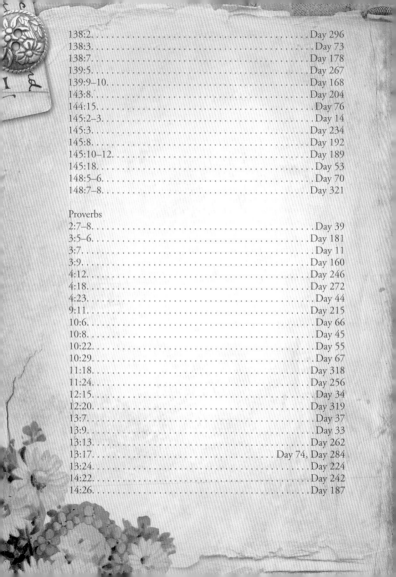